The

ORGANIC ROSE GARDEN

Also by Liz Druitt

Landscaping with Antique Roses
(with G. Michael Shoup)

The
ORGANIC
ROSE
GARDEN

Liz Druitt

PHOTOGRAPHY BY
VIRGINIA BROWN

TAYLOR TRADE PUBLISHING

Lanham • New York • Dallas • Boulder• Toronto • Oxford

Published by Taylor Trade Publishing
An imprint of The Rowman & Littlefield Publishing Group, Inc.
4501 Forbes Boulevard, Suite 200
Lanham, Maryland 20706

Distributed by NATIONAL BOOK NETWORK

The Library of Congress cataloged the hardcover edition of this book as:

Druitt, Liz.
    The organic rose garden / Liz Druitt : photography by Virginia
Brown.
        p. cm.
    Includes bibliographical references (p. 203) and index.
    1. Rose culture. 2. Roses. 3. Organic gardening. I. Title.
SB411.D74 1996
635.9'33372—dc20   95-51682

ISBN 1-58979-066-9 (pbk.: alk. paper)

Manufactured in the United States of America.
⊖™ The paper used in this publication meets the minimum requirements of
American National Standard for Information Sciences—Permanence of
Paper for Printed Library Materials, ANSI/NISO Z39.48–1992.

To all practical gardeners who love roses:
OMNE TULIT PUNCTUM QUI MISCUIT UTILE DULCI . . .
("He has carried every vote who has combined the useful with the pleasing . . .")

CONTENTS

ACKNOWLEDGMENTS

MOST OF WHAT I NOW KNOW about rose gardening was shared by rosarians and gardeners who've helped to educate me since I discovered my passion for roses ten years ago. No other group of people in the world could possibly be as friendly, supportive, and tolerant of anyone interested in learning, and any mistakes I've made in the text are in spite of their sound advice. I want to thank especially the rosarians of the Texas Rose Rustlers, the Dallas Area Historical Rose Group, the Heritage Roses Group, the New Orleans Old Garden Rose Society, and in particular my colleagues in the Heritage Rose Foundation. Some of the people who have given aid, inspiration, or both beyond all reasonable expectation are:

Martha Alejandro, Mary Anderson, Dr. Robert Basye, Virginia Brown, Benigno Diaz, John Dromgoole, Henry Flowers, Gloria Guajardo, Janet Handley and Jim Bade, Esper K. Chandler, Carol Hendricks, Carlyle Holland, Domenique and Charles Inge, Daniel P. Jones, Ruth Knopf, Dr. Yan Ma, Dr. Malcolm Manners, Coleman Mills, Ken McFarland, Holly McGuire, Brent Pemberton, Pam Puryear, Ted Rogers, Stephen Scaniello, Margaret Sharpe, G. Michael Shoup, Rosemary Sims, Angie and Leslie Smith, Conrad Tips, Leonard Veazey, Charles A. Walker Jr., Dr. William C. Welch, Jane White, Brent Wiseman, Elizabeth Rice Winston, Dr. Bill Wolverton, Joe Woodard, Nellie and Ron Zimmerman, the staff of The Organic Plant Institute (Peaceable Kingdom School), the staff of the Antique Rose Emporium, the staff (especially the Grounds Division) at the American Rose Center, and all the wonderful friends who have swapped stories, dug beds, and hunted roses with me.

FOREWORD

ELIZABETH RICE WINSTON
Founder of The Organic Plant Institute

IT'S A LUCKY THING we don't know something's impossible when we set out to do it. In 1970, having just moved here to the country, I first took sharpshooter shovel in hand to remove twenty-four inches of red clay from the area in front of the little farmhouse. My intention was to start a garden, but it was August, in the middle of a serious drought, and most of the land was hard to tell from the road due to overgrazing. I was very much on my own at the time. There wasn't even telephone service during those early years and the road to the local barbecue, bar, and grocery (all one business) in Washington-on-the-Brazos, where the pay phone was, became impassable except by tractor when it rained.

The whole art of gardening is experience. Already an organic gardener, I set out to bring back the land that cotton, cattle, and thoughtless management by previous owners had destroyed. Many hours were spent on the back of Teddie, the venerable tractor, pulling a disc and throwing seeds of vetch and winter rye over my shoulders. Of course, I made my share of mistakes, but some of those led to learning. When I discovered the hard way that everything edible had to be kept in airtight jars, I scattered a weevil-infested fifty pound sack of black-eyed peas in the orchard and found out they were also an excellent cover crop. The land responded and became fertile again, given time and rain. Four years later a local rancher told me, "If I'd known all that grass was here, I'd have bought it myself." A lot has happened both in the world of agriculture and on these particular 152 acres since then.

The "I" became "we" and finally "it," as general interest in organic gardening and ecological preservation grew. In 1972, the Peaceable Kingdom Foundation was charted as a non-profit school, finally resulting in The Organic Plant Institute. By 1976, with the aid of the University of Texas Rare Plant Study Center, we had an herbarium containing 450 pressed blooming species of plants indigenous to the land. We also had rich, hand-dug organic gardens, both vegetable and ornamental. This was in spite of the fact that most people still thought growing organically was right up there with communism and seeing flying saucers, and continued to do so until the late 1980s, when state certification began. Texas now has the most powerful organic certification laws in the country.

We always had a few roses around the grounds, mostly favorites remembered from my childhood, like 'Yellow Lady Banks'', 'Peace', and the wonderful red Floribunda from our neighbor, Lillie Lathan, which turned out to be 'Eutin'. My first real awakening to roses, however, was caused by another hand-me-down plant, this one from my friends, the Harpers. Mrs. Harper objects to roses because they are thorny. This particular one had survived as long as it had only because it was beneath notice and had come with the house. It was stuck in the ground under a fig tree at the side of a two-story tin building, not being worthy of garden space. I saw it bloom once, myself, and was not impressed by the rather measly specimen. I accepted it politely, however, when offered the chance to transplant it from Houston to The Organic Plant Institute.

We planted it in good soil, of course, and it got rain run-off from the roof, but otherwise it was left to languish, which it didn't. The next spring, it was two stories high, spread from eave to eave, and covered with beautiful, fragrant, pink-and-white flowers. Enter Liz Druitt, whom I had looked up as someone who knew about roses. She identified this enthusiastic plant as 'Fun Jwan Lo', a Shrub rose that had been imported into this country from China in the 1920s for use as a vigorous rootstock. Its vigor certainly impressed me, and so did the world of hardy roses that she introduced to me. Roses are in all of my gardens now, and have become a necessary part of my life. In Navasota, cardinals nest in the climbing Polyantha "Cécile Brünner" on the porch pillar of my house, and I've discovered some handsome Rugosas that tolerate our salty water. At my house on the school grounds, the Large-flowered Climbers 'Silver Moon' and 'New Dawn' ramble from the resting place of my beloved dog Lazlo, who was half coyote. What could be a more fitting tribute?

In exchange, I was able to show Liz the organic growing techniques that helped her avoid the toxic sprays she so disliked. She came and managed the ornamental gardens for The Organic Plant Institute for three years, trying out many combinations of roses with other plants in various successful designs. As far as we can tell, it's a myth that roses can't be grown organically. Roses are now everywhere on the Institute's grounds, almost 300 specimens chosen for their ability to adapt without chemical aid to our soils and growing conditions. The color, fragrance, and flavor of roses is enhanced by organic culture, and how nice to be able to stroll through a safe garden, grazing on fat, tart rose hips as you go.

There are so many sensible advantages to growing roses this way. The available chemicals are expensive, unpleasant to use, and toxic to the life in and above the soil. Without them there's no worry that you, your children, or your dog will track poison from the rose garden into the house, onto the rug where the baby is playing. An organic garden is an education in the wisdom of nature, and this education is easily obtained by enjoyable observation—as has always been true, "the best fertilizer is the gardener's shadow." There are may ways—very possible ways—to feed, nurture, and protect roses in a healthy garden. That is what this book is about.

The

ORGANIC ROSE GARDEN

ROSES IN PERSPECTIVE

Flashes of color on a green bush catch your eye from a distance. As an addicted rose hunter, you're drawn to the site immediately, whether on foot or in your vehicle. A little closer and you can tell if the flowers just belong to a camellia, or if you've really found a rose. By the time you reach the bush you'll often know which cultivar it's likely to be. There are a certain number of roses that turn up everywhere, in every nook and garden cranny, all over the South. Maybe this one will be something new—to you—and you'll get that extra excitement, but it really doesn't matter. Every time you see one of these lovely creatures in a new situation you add to your store of information about them and how they grow in all sorts of circumstances. Above all, you learn what remarkable performers they are when treated like regular plants, because these gardens—or cemeteries, or abandoned home sites—are rarely the epitome of suburban perfection. The chemical lawn fertilizer, the clinically pruned shrubs, and, above all, the supporting arsenal of rose sprays are conspicuously absent.

These commonly found roses survive in an imperfect world, managing on a diet of dirt and water, with maybe some tossed-out coffee grounds and the thoughtful donations of a passing cat or dog. As long as choking weeds are kept back and sunlight is available, they seem to be willing to fight like berserkers to live and bloom. You can't avoid wondering if all the help we feel compelled to give them is really necessary, especially when the names of these ubiquitous varieties are noted. Perhaps sixty percent of the time the rugged rose will be an Old Garden Rose as defined by the American Rose Society, belonging to one of the many rose classes developed before the introduction of the first Hybrid Tea in 1867. Certainly these cultivars would seem to have an excuse, by arriving before modern technology, for being so sturdy. The rest of the group, however, are "modern" roses: Floribundas such as 'Valentine' and 'Eutin', Hybrid Musks like 'Belinda', uncountable Polyanthas from 'Clotilde Soupert' to 'The Fairy', lots of Large-flowered Climbers like 'New Dawn', and Shrub roses like the foundling study-named "Katy Road Pink," Miniatures ('Red Cascade' is everywhere) and *Rosa rugosa rubra*, even Hybrid Teas such as 'Radiance' or 'Tropicana'. These roses have some years on them and they've been around a lot of gardens, but they are by no means ancient history.

To understand why the roses do so well in natural conditions it's helpful to know a little bit about the actual history of roses and humans and what has happened in gardens in the last two hundred years. Roses are much older than that and the effect of their beauty on people has been recorded for at least three millennia, but the number of them available and their accessibility for every type of gardening are fairly recent phenomena. Plant breeding in general didn't take off until after Linnaeus' studies of plants' sexual reproduction startled so many narrow-minded botanists and stimulated deliberate hybridization programs in the mid-1700s.

By the end of that century the number of roses available had expanded significantly for the first time in human experience. At the same time, many European nations were expanding both their territories and their trade boundaries, in a contest for economic dominion. The opening of China for trade—though against her will—made the most difference to the roses. There were a remarkable number both of species (wild roses) and cultivars (garden hybrids) in China, and plant hunters brought a representative selection back to Europe during the early 1800s. These roses were adapted to a warm climate where long periods of dormancy served no purpose and constantly repeated flowering cycles increased the possibility of reproduction and survival. When the Chinese roses were crossed with the cold hardy, once-blooming European varieties, on the second cross their recessive gene for remontancy came to the fore. Suddenly (in historic terms) roses were everywhere, blooming repeatedly with varying degrees of cold or heat tolerance, remarkably different types of flowers and wonderful combinations of fragrance.

This is where the sorting-out process had to start. Early rose breeders were no more or less conscientious than those of our time. As a result there were a lot of excellent varieties produced—and even more failures. Thousands and thousands of roses from the nineteenth century didn't make it into the twentieth, through various combinations of poor luck and poor health. The ones that did make it, numbering in the mere hundreds, had to

The understated beauty
of roses. Here, *Rosa
rugosa rubra.*

have the gift of physical sturdiness—at least for their particular location—supplemented by an ability to inspire human affection. A handful, like 'Old Blush', the main China rose parent, would have made it anyway because of wide adaptability, easy fertility and heavy planting on several continents. For most of the roses, however, survival included piggyback rides from place to place under the care of some human who was fond of them.

Roses are tough, but they're not without needs. As new young cuttings they require a constant supply of moisture and a little protection from direct sun in order to start a new set of roots. When those roots reach planting size the baby bushes need adequate water when it doesn't rain, plenty of sun and rich soil to feed their eager appetites. To reach their personal best and maintain it they will continue to need these things all their lives, which can be very, very long. (There's at least one rose specimen on record that's already 500 years old. A well-maintained rose bush should be around to give pleasure to your great grandchildren, if nobody paves over it in the meantime.) Whether they can make it on their own or not, all roses will benefit from some tending by humans, particularly as immature plants, if they're going to thrive. The most fascinating aspect of rose gardening, to me, is that humans have always been so willing to give them this care. *Our* species is plain addicted to *their* species, and that's the main reason we have so many of the old varieties of roses lingering in our gardens today.

Even before the technological advances of the nineteenth century, devoted gardeners were hand carrying their little cuttings of this and that wherever humans migrated and settled. Fragrance has a powerful hold on

From formal gardens to casual backyard decor, roses make any setting beautiful.

us, evoking strong memories more efficiently than any other of the five senses, and the scent of a favorite rose can thus be used as a doorway through time and distance. For long voyages, or oxcart trips across the North American continent, rose cuttings were packed away in any moisture holding material such as Spanish moss or sawdust in hopes that a percentage of them would survive. Some cuttings, already rooted into an available receptacle, would actually be hand-watered and nursed over several thousand hardscrabble miles. (My favorite method of rose transportation has always been the cutting stuck into the potato. I read about this and immediately saw the value of this neatly portable moisture source, so I set out to try and reproduce the method. I purchased several potatoes from the grocery, sliced them in half and inserted cuttings of 'Old Blush', with the idea that it would root if any rose could. By the next morning all of the cuttings were deader than if I'd left them drying on the kitchen counter. I'd forgotten that commercial potatoes are treated with a growth retardant to keep them from sprouting inconveniently. A little old lady subsequently told me that she'd done it often and it worked well—if you use homegrown potatoes.)

By the mid 1800s it was much easier to transport large quantities of plants, both overseas and across the continent. Wardian glass cases, which were essentially portable greenhouses, had been developed in England to protect consignments of plants on board sailing ships from salt water and drying wind. This allowed the nursery business to expand profitably to any major port city—Charleston, Mobile and New Orleans are just some of the locations that were served by nationally known nurserymen. From seaports plants were transported up rivers on barges or steamboats, perhaps the most uncertain leg of the journey. In spite of their romantic history, steamboats were often poorly built and on the verge of blowing up or dropping apart. Thomas Affleck, a horticulturist who expanded his Mississippi nursery into Central Texas, lost an entire shipment of plants in a steamboat disaster. Nonetheless he made a public boast that any rose introduced in France one year could be in his nursery only a year later. Sadly for romance, but with good results for safe transportation, the railroad lines had crossed the continent by the end of the 1850s. This opened up the interior cities to the nursery trade and gave gardening a huge boost, bringing significant numbers of roses and other plants into all parts of the country.

Just when gardening reached twin peaks of popularity and plant availability, the Civil War brought everything to a crashing halt. If you wonder why there are so many plants from antebellum days lingering in the South, you can thank the warm climate, but also keep some gratitude for the Northern blockade that cut off trade with the outside world for several years. The war that devastated human fortunes and lives was actually quite useful for those of us who are interested in the survival of hardy roses. What there was when the war started was *all* there was for a long time, and the habit of conservation and self-sufficiency developed in desperation at that time has never completely died out. The rural South in particular has never caught up financially with its early days of wealth, and as a result plant-sharing is as widely practiced now as it ever was. The date and name on a rose bush are not as important here as is the need to have it grow okay without store-bought extras and propagate easily to pass on to the neighbors.

There is balance in all things, so the admirable trait of conservation of existing resources has an opposite side. Another Southern quirk that supports the presence of many hand-me-down roses is the result of the former richness of the soil. The combination of warm climates and unending acres of virgin land to the West allowed shortsighted plantation owners to drag crop after crop from their fields without ever doing anything to maintain fertility. The information was available—*The American Cotton Planter* was a regularly published periodical in the mid-1800s that strongly supported the most intensive organic farming methods. The publisher of that journal called

These 'Old Blush' roses have been growing at this plantation home for more than sixty years.

for use of various green manures, lime, ground bones, compost and other familiar materials to replenish the land used for cotton and other crops. Thomas Affleck, in his almanac from 1860, commands that gardeners "accumulate manure, bones, lime-rubbish or marl, oyster shells, ashes, soot, etc., all of which are excellent . . . " He also describes mulching "with dung or coarse litter, straw or leaves, half-rotten bagasse or saw-dust, to restrain evaporation and preserve moisture . . . first stirring the surface after applying a dressing of rich compost, and . . . giving a thorough soaking of weak liquid manure, such as table-yard drainings or soap suds . . . " His almanac offers bone dust for manure at two cents the pound, ditto on super-phosphate of lime, with phosphate of Peruvian guano going at two and ¾ cents. He obviously knew what he was doing, but as with any useful advice some people followed it and the majority didn't: our fertile topsoil is pretty well gone with the wind and the rain, or trampled to concrete by the compacting hooves of livestock.

The abundance of artificial fertilizers that do nothing for the living soil is a fairly recent occurrence, the outgrowth of industrial development from the world wars. Both this and the widespread use of broad-spectrum pesticides that badly alter the natural insect pest/predator relationship are showing signs of falling from commercial favor as it becomes obvious that they have uncertain long-term value: pests mutate so rapidly to accommodate poisons. It's even possible now to find environmentally sound cockroach killers at Wal-Mart, so it seems that the organic future, revived from the ghost of the organic past, is just around the corner.

Obviously, gardening is subject to wide fluctuations in the application of common sense, and just as obviously, not everything from the past is automatically good. There was a time when Londoners didn't have too much trouble with blackspot because smog from coal fumes was so heavy it smothered fungus spores. Rose sprays of the last century often featured lead or arsenic as a main ingredient. The commonly advertised Bordeaux mixture, in use since 1878 for controlling fungus and some insect pests, is based on copper compounds which irritate eyes and skin and can be toxic to plant tissue if not precisely applied. Not everything natural is necessarily good, either. Garlic is a fine pest-repelling and anti-fungal companion plant for roses in the garden, but the highly-touted organic garlic spray is so potent it can decimate populations of beneficial insects along with pests, leaving the environment further out of balance. You still see tobacco spray offered as a natural replacement for those "bad" modern chemicals, but it outdoes many new formulas in being dangerously toxic to gardeners as well as pests. I saw a TV mystery not long ago where the murder was done with just a few drops of concentrate of tobacco applied to the victim's unprotected skin. Not something you really want to handle—I'd rather play with fire ants!

You don't need to be either an environmental fanatic or a technological wizard to successfully grow roses—just a gardener. Growing them organically is a matter of taste and practicality. If you don't like the smell, touch, or impact of the available chemicals, and if you want to make your garden a rich and vital place, going organic is a sound solution. You don't even have to be thorough about it. If you mix and match chemical and natural means (a method called Integrated Pest Management or IPM), you'll still be better off than you were—just don't eat your roses yet. Most roses can handle fairly passive organic care as well as the intensely active kind, and a remarkable number are already doing it. (In my garden they get both and like it.) A little hoeing and weeding, the sorts of things that might take time but won't cost money, are still the basic cultural practices of the Southern rural gardener. Stamp a few canes into the

'Paul Neyron' and 'Blue Mist'

clay to start some new stock and there you are—a rose garden. Those roses that can't take it will disappear, just as they did in the nineteenth century, and we won't have to worry about them.

Roses in general are strong and wonderful plants, and there are colors, shapes and sizes available to suit every gardener's taste. If, like the majority of gardeners, you'd enjoy sharing your life with some roses, I hope you can use the information in this book to select varieties that both please you and suit your needs—and that you make yourself a beautiful rose garden where you and they will thrive in good health.

PREPARING
THE WAY

If there were commandments associated with organic gardening, the first and greatest of these would be "Honor thy soil!" Care of the roses themselves must take second place to care of the soil in which they grow if you want a healthy garden. Most of us are not gifted with perfect garden soil, which would be equal parts sand, topsoil, and organic material. But good soil is, literally, the basis of all good gardening and an absolute requirement for good organic gardening. You can scrounge your plants, scavenge your building materials, even forget to fertilize now and then, but the one part of gardening to which everyone should sincerely pay attention is in the development and maintenance of the soil.

I spent eight years gardening in solid red clay that went down about three feet before it struck a layer of sand. I've spent the last several years gardening in pure sugar sand that goes about three feet down and then hits clay. As a result I'm in the habit of mixing my own garden soil because I've never had any alternative, and like any gardener I've developed favorite recipes. In clay, I added to the existing "soil" equal portions of builder's sand (not home-dug river sand—that's full of silt and inclined to compacting) and composted pine bark. It's important to use the dirt that you've got as part of the recipe—especially in clay—otherwise, when the rose roots grow out of the perfect little bed and hit reality they can go into a kind of shock, losing vitality until they learn to adjust. I also sprinkled in a leavening of gypsum in the initial preparation to loosen the particles of the clay itself over time. Well-mixed with a shovel or hoe, the resulting garden beds were

These 'Sally Holmes' and 'Tropicana' roses bloom exquisitely in mulched raised beds.

mounded about six to eight inches above the surrounding pathways—a crucial necessity for drainage in clay or limestone country. A freshly prepared bed will subside at least twenty percent during the first year, but constant mulching with organic materials will keep it both balanced in texture and raised to a proper level.

I chose composted pine bark as the organic ingredient not because of the word "composted"—the piles from which it comes are pretty well leached of live microbes and most nutrients, and also of the turpines that might hinder plant growth. Timbering and pulp-making for paper were nearby industries, so the pine bark was not prohibitively expensive. In a rice growing area I probably would use rice hulls, or cottonseed meal where cotton is grown—whatever was available in bulk. I like the dark color and slight anti-fungal properties of the bark, but it makes more sense to work with economical and renewable local supplies than to fuss over any one type of organic ingredient—they all add vital tilth and nutrient-holding texture to the soil. If you have doubts about what's available or how safe it is to use, contact your agricultural extension agent and your gardening neighbors. They can advise about things like mushroom compost, for example, which is often too "hot" and salty to use until it's been recomposted, then makes a great amendment.

In the sandy soil I've tried to borrow judicious amounts of loamy topsoil from the surrounding woods—without depleting any one area of its vital

Well-prepared soil will give you the best returns. (*The Organic Plant Institute*)

covering—and relied on mass quantities of bark, leaves, and pine needles that have been shredded by the lawn mower to make up a largely organic mixture. Pine trees are not just a regional resource here, they loom over my garden on every side. In exchange for the sunlight they block, the least they can do, as I see it, is donate materials to my beds. Even though this is cheaper than my previous preparation recipe, it has the drawbacks of requiring more intensive labor and of stealing a lot of nitrogen from the beds as the uncomposted materials break down. Every gardener can work out the pros and cons of various local materials for themselves, as long as they stick to the basic three-part balance of ingredients.

Both clay and sand appear to eat organic material, but sand eats it faster, like a shark in a feeding frenzy. If you don't mix in plenty at the start and keep it well topped-off with mulch, your garden beds may appear innocent of amendments by the end of four or five months. It's almost scary in the beginning, but over a few years' time this ravenous appetite will slow down to a slight but constant case of the munchies.

Roses like richly organic soil. They are necessarily heavy feeders to support growing and blooming on such an energetic scale over such a long season. Given a choice, they seem to prefer clay-based soils that hold nutrients longer and give firm support to their rather shallow root systems. They will thrive in most situations, however, if given an adequate selection of favorite foods and the right pH so that the microbes on their roots are able to break down the required nutrients and absorb them for use. A pH of 6.0, slightly acidic, is probably ideal, but most roses are comfortable anywhere from 5.5 up to neutral 7.0. Tea roses and particularly China roses seem able to thrive even in rather alkaline soils, as do individuals of many classes. If you live in a notably alkaline situation (water quality can matter almost as much as soil conditions), ask your rose-growing neighbors which varieties have proven successful for them. There are soil-testing kits available at many nurseries to help determine pH on a regular basis, but if your soil is well prepared in the beginning and well maintained over time, you'll probably find that it stays within the acceptable range. Regular additions of live compost and occasional watering with compost tea are additionally helpful in balancing the pH to the most comfortable level for your roses.

$\mathscr{H}$OW TO TAKE A SOIL TEST

To prepare a soil sample, you'll want a plastic bucket (to avoid contamination with zinc or lead), a shovel, a trowel and some extra strength zip-type plastic bags that hold up to a pint. If your garden is more or less uniform in its behavior, one soil test will serve for the whole area. If, on the other hand, you have special problems in specific areas, you'll want to test that soil separately and not mix it in with the rest of the sample. To get the sample you first dig a tidy hole about twelve inches deep in the chosen location—this depth is to ensure you get material from the area where the majority of your roots will be growing. (Some labs suggest only a six-inch depth, but that's not really adequate for good information if you're growing roses, other flowering shrubs, bulbs or woody perennials.) Once you have a hole slightly wider than your shovel, use the blade to slice off a clean slab about one inch thick from one side, all the way down. Use the trowel to scrape away both edges of this slab from the shovel blade, until you're left with a "core" in the center about one inch thick by one inch wide. Dump this in your plastic bucket, and move on to the next site. Take a minimum of four "cores" this way, though a large garden will be better tested by taking more—roughly eight per acre. Deposit them all in your bucket and mix them up *thoroughly* with your trowel, removing any foreign objects such as roots, leaves, rocks, etc. From this mixture, take out between one half and one whole pint (labs vary in their requirements—check first) and package this composite representative sample in the plastic bag, carefully labeled with your name and address. That's part one of your soil test.

Part two consists of either filling out a form, if you've been sent one, or writing a note that explains what your test area is used for (i.e. garden, orchard), whether you grow organically, what sort of plants you are growing now, any problems you may be having, what you hope to do with the area in the future, and where you live—what county, nearby cities, etc. The more thorough this information, the better job the lab can do of interpreting the numbers in your analysis.

A routine soil test takes about five working days and will include information about pH, salinity and the three major nutrients: nitrogen, potassium, and phosphorus. Organic gardeners will probably want to ask for micronutrients to be tested as well, to get a more complete range of information. Then the lab will send you the test results, plus any recommendations they may care to make about fertilizers or specific problem-solving. Test costs currently range from ten dollars for the base analysis, up to about twenty-five dollars for a complete study, depending also upon whether you use a private company or a university laboratory. If you're not familiar with a lab already, your county extension agent can send you all the information you need for just a phone call.

$\mathcal{H}$OW TO MAKE COMPOST

Compost is not a plain heap of horse manure, or an old leaf pile. It's a living soil: a moist, dark, nutrient-rich product with a fine earthy odor and a load of fully active beneficial bacteria. Even a small amount added as you plant, or worked into the surface of the garden bed, will help fix a problem in soil texture by aiding the breakdown of heavy clay soils, and by adding nutrient and water retention to sandy soils. A wonderful aspect of compost is that its live organisms spread into the surrounding soil to improve it, sort of like sourdough starter. Live compost helps balance the pH of your existing soil, and it's full of nutrients that improve plant vigor, cutting down on the need for supplementary fertilizers and substantially increasing resistance to insects and diseases. Compost tea, made from a scoop of fresh compost soaked in water overnight (ratios of compost to water can vary with your preference, as can the amount of time you let it soak), is a quick pick-me-up for ailing roses. It also has a reputation for slowing down the development of fungal diseases. The benefits of live compost more than outweigh the effort involved in making it.

To make a compost pile, you'll need a shovel or hoe and a hose or other water source. It's also useful to have a compost thermometer, available at many nurseries or through gardening catalogs, to monitor the rising and falling temperatures of the pile. You don't have to have a bin of any kind, though using one makes a tidier looking pile and can help protect your work from animals digging for choice decaying "treats" or kitties burrowing into a warm place for a snooze.

Choose a level spot near a water source, preferably in the shade, and clear it of grass and weed cover by scraping them off with a sharp shovel so that your pile will contact the micro-organisms in the ground. Put down a three inch layer of **carbon**, this is brown, dry, coarse stuff like dead leaves, straw, chipped-up branches and twigs. Then add a one-inch layer of **nitrogen**, moist organic material like fresh grass clippings, dried or fresh manure, and kitchen vegetable scraps. Try not to add meat or fat because those will attract predators to the pile, from raccoons to houseflies. Also, watch out for large quantities of weed seeds—most will be sterilized by the heat of the composting process, but it's better not to count on it. Scatter a dusting of regular soil and a little organic fertilizer like blood and bone meal over the top of each layer and then moisten it with the hose. Once you've got the basic proportions adjusted, you can stir the layers you've just created together and start on the next level. It's important that all the ingredients end up evenly moistened but not soggy—if the pile gets too wet the living organisms can drown.

The best size for a pile is roughly four feet by four feet across and about three feet high, so keep adding, moistening, and stirring alternate layers of carbon and nitrogen until that size is reached. When the pile is finished, protect it from leaching rains and moisture loss with a loose covering of straw. You can rake this off and re-use it whenever you turn your pile, or work it into another pile. If you don't have straw or leaves or some other non-seedy (boy, can those seeds sprout on top of a compost pile—especially tomatoes!) organic covering, you can use a tarp or plastic sheet loosely fastened over the top to shelter the pile.

A well-made compost pile heats up in a few days to between 130° and 150° Fahrenheit, showing that the bacteria are alive and at work inside. You can turn and remoisten the pile once a week or once a month—the more often you turn it and the more finely shredded your starting materials are, the faster you get results. Much has been written about the use of biodynamic compost starter, and this stuff honestly does make some difference in the speed and quality of your results. However, so does a regular addition of good old urine, either poured on from a collection jar or directly applied, if you have the right personal equipment for the chore. Urine is quickly transformed by the microbes into a sanitary, odorless source of nitrogen, which the composting process requires in quantity. It's cheaper than any store-bought starter and you can never add too much.

When the materials are almost completely decomposed, the pile is ready to use. A finished pile is dark, moist, and looks much like humus from the forest floor. It won't heat up anymore, and you shouldn't be able to recognize the original ingredients: if you can tell it was a zucchini, you're not through turning. If your compost is not finished all the way it can continue heating up when applied to the garden beds, which is okay in winter for early vegetable starts, but hard on roses in the middle of a hot summer. Also, the composting process burns nitrogen, so raw organic materials in the garden mean extra applications of nitrogen to keep soil levels balanced.

Try to keep finished compost covered in the pile and mulch over any compost added to a garden bed, so that it doesn't dry out and let the valuable bacteria die. Even dead compost is a wonderful organic supplement for soil tilth, but the living product is exceptional.

MULCH

The idea of covering a garden bed with an insulating layer of coarse material is ancient—and still completely sound. This layer, which only needs to be about one inch deep to be effective, acts to keep the soil warmer in winter and cooler in summer. It also protects the surface of the soil beneath it,

This 'Martha Gonzales' rose has been mulched with straw; coarse bark is on the path.

keeping living compost organisms moist and shaded, and preventing compaction of the soil. Water and nutrients penetrate better when mulch is used, and weeds come out easier because their roots can't grab tight hold in the loose material. Mulch gradually decays in a slow composting process, so it needs to be replaced at least each spring and fall—more often if you see the soil beneath starting to show, or if you live in a very cold or hot zone where the roses want the extra protection in either summer or winter. An unsung benefit of mulch is that it can protect public plantings from mechanical damage caused by maintenance equipment. Specimen roses in particular, planted in cemeteries or other public areas, are subject to lawn mower "tilt" and weed-eater girdling. Death from conscientious maintenance can be prevented or reduced by regular applications of attractive mulch material so that weeds and grass don't grow close to the base of the rose bush. A tip from the volunteers trying to preserve the many old roses in the Natchez City Cemetery is to mulch in squares in public areas, so that the lawn mowers can work around the bushes with the least amount of difficulty.

The material you use for mulch affects the speed of decomposition. A fine, rapidly decomposing mulch like shredded bark will go much more quickly than chunks of the same material. Old mulch can be turned into the bed as an organic amendment when it's time to apply a new layer. If the mulch material is not completely decomposed, make sure to add extra nitrogen on a regular basis to replace the nitrogen used in the composting process.

Anything that will protect the soil can be used as mulch, but like any gardener, I have my favorites. I like the barks, particularly composted pine bark, because of the groomed appearance it gives a bed and because of the slight antifungal properties it adds. Chunky bark is more useful if you have trouble with slugs or pillbugs, making it more difficult for them to hide in the bed itself. Rice hulls, pine straw, regular straw (not hay, unless it's salt, or coastal, hay with no seeds) or any organic material will work, even layers of newspaper or brown cardboard. The last two aren't ideal, because they don't allow good penetration of water and fertilizers, but they make great weed barriers and decompose usefully. Avoid bleached cardboard, because it releases dioxins as it breaks down. Also avoid pecan hulls and walnut hulls: they look great, but the tannin levels they contain are very hard on plant life. Both of them work well in the pathways, however, and help keep down weeds. Corn gluten can be added to the mulch material as an extra nutrient for the roses and as a safe weed prohibitor—for some reason it works very well to keep seedlings from sprouting. (Don't use it if you're sowing annual seeds into the same bed!)

Regular mulching is an important element of basic soil maintenance and a vital part addition to continued soil fertility. In protecting and feeding the soil, mulch also protects and eventually feeds the roses that the soil supports.

MAKING A ROSE BED

The actual process of building a bed for roses is fairly simple, but it does require some initial labor. A well-made garden bed takes less work with every succeeding year, so it's worth doing thoroughly in the beginning.

If you're starting with a virgin site, you will have already determined that it gets the four to six hours of direct sun that roses require for good blooming and good health, and that there's a water source within a reasonable distance. After laying out the shape of the bed with a garden hose or stakes and string, use a sharp shovel to scrape off the layer of grass or weeds to a depth of about two inches—deep enough to get the majority of the roots. Prepare the soil as described at the beginning of this chapter, working any existing topsoil into the recipe and making sure the resulting mixture mounds up at least six inches above the surface of the ground.

Unless your bed is in an area completely surrounded by paving or gravel, you'll want to put in flashing at this point to prevent grass or weeds from creeping back into the bed. Flashing is rigid metal or plastic sheeting that acts as a barrier wall to keep invaders out and help soil amendments stay in. It's available from garden centers, or you can recycle old corrugated roof panels with a pair of tin snips. I live in an area of mole activity, so I use flashing that is twenty-four inches wide, sinking eighteen inches of that below the soil and leaving six inches above to stop grubbing armadillos. If you don't have this sort of visitor, twelve inches below ground will control most roots, with only two inches necessary above. Well-prepared garden soil doesn't wash away easily, especially if it's properly protected with mulch, so the flashing isn't absolutely necessary to keep the soil in the bed though it does help a little. To install the flashing, use a flat-bladed shovel to wedge a trench to the required depth all the way around the bed. Lay in the flashing, firm up the trench, and you're done. Metal or plastic showing above ground can be easily hidden by decorative edging materials. Any edging that is in harmony

A drip irrigation system built in under your rose bed provides excellent moisture control.

with your house and suits your tastes is fine; unless you're building a retaining wall/terrace bed or a high raised bed, the edging is not really a structural necessity, so it doesn't have to be all that sturdy. Most organic gardeners today choose only to avoid treated timbers for garden bed edging, as the arsenic and other chemicals used in the treatment have been shown to leach somewhat into the soil.

The only other vital step in bed building is the placement of an irrigation system if you're going to install one permanently. Obviously, pipes for drip irrigation have to be laid under or over a flashing barrier—your choice depends on how permanent you think the bed will be. If you're not certain, leave the pipe on top and cover it with mulch if you don't like looking at it. Soaker hoses can also be laid directly on the surface of the soil, then hidden with mulch. After you've built the bed and planned your irrigation system, you're essentially ready to start playing with the roses.

DESIGNING THE ROSE GARDEN

When you set out to create a garden it's very rare to start with a completely blank page. Most of us are dealing with an already existing space, a preset territory that we own or rent and can't easily change. Also, if you're far enough along in gardening to have any idea of deliberate design plans, you probably have a number of plants—specific roses among them—that *must* be included because you can't imagine doing without them. With those two givens, there are still a number of variables to take into account, possibilities to explore—and difficulties to overcome.

BASIC DESIGN PRINCIPLES

I don't think there can be any rigid rules in rose garden design, because I can't imagine looking at a garden that makes someone happy and telling them it's *wrong*—no matter whether I like it or not myself. The mere involvement of an active, creative gardener will make any garden pleasurable to see. There are, however, certain elements that can heighten the visual pleasure received from any garden—growing organically doesn't mean giving up beauty. Some of those elements that make a significant difference are framing, accenting certain areas, and adding levels of height. Another genuinely important element of garden design is comfort, making the garden physically appealing to the person or people who will use it. Organic gardening is a critical part of this element, in that it makes the whole garden environment a healthier, safer, and more pleasurable place in which to spend your time. A final aspect of design to consider is creativity or inventiveness. There are many ways to use roses beyond those with which we are traditionally familiar. Designing a garden rather than just sticking the plants haphazardly in the ground offers an opportunity to go beyond the limits of habit or custom and create new patterns both of beauty and of function.

Not every garden needs to have all the elements discussed here, but knowing some basic techniques of design will help you decide what matters most to you, and what type of rose garden will best meet your needs. Established rose gardens can be expanded or modified to accommodate some of these design elements as well. The most important thing, always, is to make sure you've pleased yourself and will enjoy and use the result.

Most design elements are based on common sense: once they've been described you wonder why you didn't notice them before, because they're pretty obvious. Framing is a good example of this. Few people hang a picture on a wall without some kind of frame, even if it's just a simple matte to improve a poster. The frame shows very clearly where your eyes should aim, a sort of "this is the picture, inside this specific space, the rest is just wall"

statement. To achieve this useful focus in the garden, the animate (living plants) is surrounded by the inanimate. The latter includes the obvious—edging—plus any fences or walls and also the pathways you may have considered simply as access to the space. Anything that concretely defines the shape of the garden and separates it from the rest of the yard is part of the frame and should be included in your developing design. This may seem like a major deviation from concentrating on roses, but it's the difference between the big picture and the little picture in your garden. Bringing plants together to make a specifically attractive grouping is certainly part of design, but stopping at that point can leave the garden as a whole looking uncomfortably chaotic and unfinished.

A good example of the value of framing is the appeal of the tradi-

LEFT: Stones are the focal point in this garden, creating a stunning contrast with the delicacy of 'Marie Pavie' and lamb's ears.

BELOW: 'Buff Beauty' cascades over the edge of a retaining wall.

'Prosperity' spills over a stone garden wall, showing the attractive effect of different levels.

tional Southern dooryard garden. Within the boundaries of the rectangular fence, neatly split by the path that runs straight to the front door, any sort of hodgepodge planting might exist. China and Tea roses, geraniums, pinks and iris, lantana, dill and four o'clocks, all of them are tucked in as space allows, or cling to life in cans and Styrofoam cups, waiting to be planted out. The fact that so many people are drawn to this crowded, messy and endearing style of gardening is dependent not just on the jumble of colors and fragrances it allows but on the rigid framework that separates it from total, incomprehensible chaos. The beds may be edged with anything from cedar shingles to bricks to upended beer bottles, but they are edged. The path may be grass, flagstone, or broken bits of driveway paving, but there is a distinct path. The fence may have deviated from classic picket or wrought iron and be simple or fancy rolled wire, but it will always be rectangular and it will always be there to separate the part which is meant to be the garden from everything around it.

Someone who raises koi, those huge ornamental carp, clarified this design concept for me perfectly. As he put it, the owner of the fish may appreciate the beauty of each individual specimen, but to the visitor it's the pattern of the whole school, moving within the frame of the pond, that's immediately visible. You may not have the ability to look over your garden from above as one does with a fish pond, but even wandering through it at eye level you can appreciate the pleasure a clearly defined frame can give. At the same time, don't forget about the little picture because you are the owner of the "fish," after all. Careful placement of specific plants that will flower together in season is one way of creating these vignettes. If you have a particular spot that is consistently of interest, you may want to use a piece of garden art to accent it and pull attention to that place. Having this kind of accent in your garden also helps in interpreting what you're seeing, just as framing does, and it can have a powerfully pleasing effect. Anything from a marble statue to a gazing ball will serve the purpose if you're traditional. Take a look at some of those neat gardens with the white-painted tires ringing the flowers, or the kind where handmade plywood garden figures show their rumps to passersby, to start getting ideas for livelier focal points. If it draws your eye, it works, and if you like it, it's art.

To reuse the aquatic metaphor in introducing a third major element of design, you can get more plants comfortably into any garden space if you think of it as a fish tank that will not be operating at capacity until it's supporting top feeders, middle feeders and bottom feeders. Plants can't move themselves about the way fish do, so it's up to you to allow for adequate light and air to penetrate each layer, but there's a great deal of available space going unused in most gardens that could very happily be filled with roses. These versatile plants are available in a remarkable range of sizes and forms and need only a little firm structural support to be lifted romantically overhead or even over the roof. This is where pillars, trellises, arbors, and arches come into the design plan. These features can be added on purpose—remembering that a mature climbing rose can be a heavy weight, and the

structures should be correspondingly stout—or used as found. Any fence or wall is potentially a rose support, as long as there's an adequate four or more hours of direct sun and some air movement, and you aren't planning on repainting for a few years. A detachable trellis can protect exterior walls and roofs, while a few discreet nails as tie-off points give a much more natural look, as if the rose were growing up the wall on its own. Grooming and training climbing roses do require a little effort, especially when ladders are involved, but the creative effects that can be achieved are beautiful and wildly varied.

As a final design note, remember that a large part of the purpose of a garden is having a pleasant space to spend time outdoors, so don't make the mistake of setting up a yard that will be all work and no play—unless that's truly what makes you happy. Be sure you plan for seating that will allow you to stop, rest,

'Dortmund' may be enjoyed on the second story as well as the first.

These old-fashioned wrought iron chairs blend with
the antiquity of 'Old Blush'.

A pillar of 'Climbing American
Beauty'—giving a dead tree new life.

A relaxed seating group with 'Betty Prior' and 'Iceberg' roses in the background.

and review the beauty of your achievements, plus any other features, such as a dining area or hammock for snoozing, that will meet your particular needs. This is true for any kind of needs, as almost everyone enjoys a garden atmosphere. The San Antonio Botanic Garden is one of many public gardens that has developed areas for folks with various physical challenges. They have a fragrance garden for visually impaired visitors where all the plants are touchable, scented, and labeled with Braille tags. Any private garden can be either retro-fitted or freshly designed to suit special needs. In addition to the above idea, raised planters (or tall containers) and firm pathways providing access for wheelchair gardeners are sensible options, and frequent seating designed as part of the whole can allow invalid or elderly gardeners to keep working and appreciating their own work. Miniature roses, groundcover types like the neat Shrub variety 'Ralph's Creeper', and "thornless" cultivars like the Polyantha 'Marie Pavié' are good choices for raised gardens in particular. A combination of creativity and common sense should work to make rose gardening possible for almost any situation.

Garden seating provides a place for you to enjoy the beauty you've created. Note how the path, its edging, and the fence in the background are framing devices.

ing. Kohlrabi is, of course, a cool season vegetable—as it is being harvested for salads and steaming and the once-blooming roses are finishing their spring season, the eggplant starts can be going into the flower beds.

Many eggplant varieties fill the kohlrabi color niche for the summer, with purple stems, lavender flowers and bulging dark purple fruit, but they grow taller and should be placed accordingly—more a middle rank plant than a front edger. If you plant them with Hybrid Tea roses that have been pruned hard, this isn't a problem. The small young vegetable plant and cut-back rose bush will give way to a taller set of everything, still perfectly proportioned. Eggplants are actually available in several colors and color mixtures. One of my favorite designs involves the Chinese long white 'Ping Tung' with the China roses such as 'Louis Philippe' and 'Ducher'. 'Louis Philippe' is a rich soft crimson, cupped and fruit-scented, on a delicately angular bush with neatly pointed foliage. 'Ducher' is one of the very few China whites, also cupped, double and fragrant, with a touch of burgundy in the canes and new growth. The sensuously slender 'Ping Tung', though borne in masses of long cream white ribbons, doesn't overpower the delicacy of these roses the way a squattier variety might. Another favorite is the Turkish eggplant that has the form, size and color, though not the foliage, of a good orange tomato. It has big, handsome, purple-tinted eggplant foliage. A double-take-causing plant on its own in a garden ("that was a *what?*"), it works to good advantage with some of the brighter modern roses—the oranges and particularly the yellows. 'Rise and Shine', a fragrant yellow miniature rose, looks very nice with a globular orange Turkish eggplant behind it and a backdrop of the dramatic new 'Oranges and Lemons' striped rose. A few of the old yellow daylilies from grandmother's garden round the picture out and are as edible and even tastier when raw than the roses.

You might think that tomatoes, with their enthusiastic growth habits, would be harder to fit into the "flower" garden. If you are not fixated on caging and training, tomatoes can be nicely soft, cascading plants of whose fruits, you get most, but not all, of. Determinate, bushy varieties can be planted toward the middle of the bed, and indeterminate vining types work either on the fence as a backdrop or flowing over the side of a large container or high raised bed. Vivid scarlet 'Showbiz' or 'Lichterloh'—especially the latter with its multitude of fat orange hips—are natural companions. Oranges like 'Tropicana' or 'Fragrant Cloud' mix well, while bright yellows, as with Turkish eggplant, go best of all. Choose a color that's close to broccoli or mustard flower yellow, such as the Floribunda 'Sunflare', and you can't go wrong. Yellow rosebuds in a tomato salad with a pepper vinaigrette dressing (many roses have a natural hint of pepper in the calyx behind the petals) are delicious for the eye as well as the pallet. Toss nasturtiums into both the planting and the recipe and you achieve glory. If you don't want that particular glory, or don't want bright colors in your garden, there is at least one tomato I've found that blends with older, softer roses. The 'Purple

Calabash', an indeterminate and wildly vigorous plant, produces fruits in a peculiar shade of brownish mauve that works oddly well with mauve pink shades like 'Rose de Rescht' or the dark crimson of 'Oklahoma'. In this case you will want to plant the roses in front of the vegetable, as you might never see them again if you let them get behind. The 'Purple Calabash' also works with white roses, and the gnarly, deeply grooved fruits make dainty flowers even more ethereal in contrast. This tomato is called "cat-faced", which, as a cat owner, I found insulting. It's an ugly fruit with a beautiful flavor and a strange fascination for the eye, but I saw no resemblance to cats in it. With time, however, and study of the feline physiognomy, I have begun to see that my cats are, after all, a bit tomato-faced.

Elephant garlic snaking through 'Eutin'.

All alliums go well with roses. The spiky leaves of garlic and chives give a focal point to spreading bushy forms, and the allium flower range of purple, white, pale yellow, and pink is a natural for most rose varieties. In addition, alliums provide insect protection and even some fungus protection if they are allowed to remain for a period of years and increase the natural sulfur content of the soil. The rose that has an onion blooming through its branches will not have as much trouble with aphids, thrips, or other predators. They have to be right up next to each other to achieve this—a leek two feet away is like no leek at all. Leeks are, in fact, one of the finest garden vegetables in appearance. Their handsome size, perennial vigor, and neatly draped gray-green leaves make them a treat in any design. Only elephant garlic really comes close in appearance, though both have very harvestable flower heads for drying. The nice thing about alliums is that they're not as limited in season as some of the other vegetables. You don't have to be pulling them out and replacing them when they're through fruiting—you can deal with them whenever you like. If today seems like a good day for Vichyssoise, it doesn't matter what the season is. You can harvest your leeks anytime. The ideal plan would be to always replace the outgoing with new plantings, like reforestation. Thus alliums of all sizes and stages are on display, while you have your bowl of pale green soup whenever you desire. A flower from the 'Green Rose', floating at the edge, will add just the perfect accent for the dish.

If the object is to protect visual rather than physical privacy, any sturdy rose bush with thick foliage will be successful—and surely more interesting than red-tip photinia. Remember to prepare the soil very well before planting, as it may be difficult to work with it once a hedge is full grown. I've seen a driveway beautifully divided by plantings of the Bourbon 'Boule de Neige' in California, and a view of the highway blocked in Texas by a mixture of *Rosa rugosa rubra* and the Hybrid Musk 'Belinda'. Unattractive foundation skirting can be hidden by roses rather than evergreens, if you like. The Hybrid Musk 'Penelope' or the Polyantha 'Marie Pavié' are two varieties that take a mixture of sun and shade and can stand up to the less than perfect soil near a house's foundation.

*I*NDIVIDUAL IDEAS

Roses have often been touted as part of a wildlife gardening plan, since their hips provide food for many species and their thick, prickly interiors are protective nesting habitat for birds. Jane White, a talented gardener and rosarian in Virginia, has taken this function and adapted it to suit her particular needs in a unique way. She has a fenced pond where she keeps a variety of ornamental ducks as a hobby, and she was frustrated by losing their eggs to marauding ravens and crows. Now she recycles roses that haven't particularly pleased her in the garden out to the edges of the pond. This way she doesn't waste the plants, and the ducks have cover and shelter for their nests. It looks colorful and interesting, especially when the ducks are gliding through the rose reflections on the still surface of the pond. She says that she didn't know the ducks would use the roses, and didn't really expect the roses to live out there, since many of them are only known as garden varieties, but the result is inspiring in a quiet way.

Naturalizing roses protect the duck eggs at this pond.

Even more inspiring for its wide-scale implications is the example of the retired NASA bioengineer, Dr. Bill Wolverton, in Picayune, Mississippi. He's using lined troughs about sixty feet long (carefully built to his patented design specifications) of plants to filter the waste from his septic system. The microbes on the plant roots purify and sterilize the water to above-EPA requirements, while the aesthetically pleasing, odorless plant system replaces the aquifer-polluting leach fields of standard septic tank installments. The vegetable garden is hidden from view of the house, much as it was in many traditional gardens, by this apparently ornamental planting. Dr. Wolverton uses butterfly ginger in his own yard because his wife likes it, but suggests that any plant or combination of plants will do an equivalent job. Even in cold climates where the roses go dormant, the root microbes continue to function efficiently. It's possible to retrofit an existing septic tank with this sort of plant technology (using Dr. Wolverton's specifications), and even more appealing to consider designing the garden space initially to take advantage of the visual and functional aspects of a waste system with a long rose hedge.

A breathtaking view of the National Cathedral as an accent for 'Bishop Darlington' in the Bishop's Herb Garden in Washington, D.C.

Rose fences can be used as dividers and partitions within a garden, but they can also be used to define or protect a garden. Inspired by staff members who insisted that roses were useless ornamental plants, Elizabeth Winston and I created a hedge at The Organic Plant Institute that works hard for its living. We used a mixture of the two red roses used most often in our harvesting for potpourri and cooking, companion planting them in a raised bed with garlic and 'Powis Castle' artemisia to reduce any health problems. Both the Floribunda 'Eutin' and the unidentified Bourbon study-named "Maggie" were grown from cuttings on site, so they cost only our time and minimal labor. Both roses were also found in gardens and re-introduced to commerce, so there's an aspect of preservation of resources as an initial function. The hedge curves around the north and east sides of the kitchen garden and works to slow the force of drying winter winds. It provides a convenient harvest location for rose petals, which are heavily used in many of the Institute's products, and a reason to have the garlic and artemisa—both additional harvest items—close to the kitchen and work areas as well. This hedge is now three years old, and except for having one young bush dug up by an overenthusiastic scratching chicken, it's had no problems and required no special care. It gets watered, fed, and mulched like any of the garden beds, and pruning is only to remove any dead wood because constant harvesting keeps the bushes low. Nearly always in bloom, this visually attractive multi-functional planting shows what roses can and should be doing.

smaller and therefore cheaper than roses grown at the point of purchase, so the occasional loss doesn't hurt as badly. Also, the shipping season for bare-root roses is during the cool weather of fall, winter, and early spring, when they can be sent more safely because they are not in a highly active stage of growth. This corresponds perfectly with the ideal planting times for us in the South. The newly received roses can go right in the ground with a minimum of frost protection and get a head start on rooting out before the next blooming season. Some nurseries ship year-round in containers, ranging in size from six inches to one gallon. These plants can be treated just like container-grown plants purchased at a local nursery; once again, they're smaller and may be more economical to buy.

When you get a bare-root rose in the mail, first check it over thoroughly for excessive shriveling from dryness or cane or root breakage. If damage is minor, this is the time to clip any bad canes or roots back to clean, healthy wood. Planting a rose with root injuries especially leaves it vulnerable to a number of diseases, such as crown gall. If there's enough damaged material to threaten the survival of the rose, let the nursery know immediately to send a replacement. You can go ahead and plant the rose—few nurseries want a corpse sent back—and try to nurse it along, but don't short yourself a rose because of shipping damage and don't wait on the call. The goal of any sensible nursery is to sell all of this season's production: when they're out of a variety, they're out until next shipping season.

After checking and cleaning up your new roses, their roots will need immediate care. I'll never forget receiving my first mail-order box of bare-root roses one afternoon from UPS. I immediately opened it and slid my dreamed-of beauties out of their plastic sleeves. They looked disconcertingly like plucked chickens: young, all trussed up neatly, roots naked of protective soil. I almost felt I should look the other way while handing them a dressing gown. But my nurturing instincts kicked in, so I untied them, cleaned them, and settled them quickly into a bucket of water to rehydrate the roots with an overnight soaking. Leaving bare-root roses in water for too long is not good for them; it does something to the quality of their roots. Anywhere from four to twenty-four hours, however, is about right for recovery after the dry period of shipping. The water can have compost tea, alfalfa, vitamin B-1 or even a handful of dirt added to it for extra benefits. Once the plants have been groomed and soaked, they're ready for immediate planting.

PROPAGATING

If you have a mother plant in mind that you wish to reproduce, there are two common ways to propagate new plants for your garden: by cuttings or by layering. (You can also create new roses from seed, but they will be different from the original variety because the genetic material in a rose seed comes from two sources: the male and the female parent. Even if you self-pollinate a variety by using two flowers from the same bush for breeding, you'll get genetic variability. Vegetative propagation—from tissue of the plant rather than seeds—ensures the same genetic variety.) Taking cuttings allows more potential plants from less material, but layering, if it's possible to do at all, is much more reliable. There are many occasions, however, when time constraints (being on the road for example, or at a public cemetery or private house, or trying to save a lovely bush from extinction by construction) don't allow for layering. Propagation by cuttings is the first and most favored way of rose reproduction, and a skill every acquisitive rose gardener should learn.

Taking a cutting is extremely easy: you just cut off a section of rose cane that's finished blooming (thus not too old, not too new) and has a few leaves and three or four axillary buds (little green bumps where the leaves join the cane) along it. Sometimes a mere three inches of cane is plenty—long cuttings don't root any better than short ones. Immediately protect the moisture level of a cutting by wrapping it in a damp paper towel and dropping it into a plastic bag. Some moisture is necessary, but too much slows down the callusing process that seals in nutrients and helps the cutting survive until new roots grow. Label the bag or a twist-on tag (if several varieties are in one bag) immediately with the name, if known, or the location, flower color, and date (it's amazing how quickly all memory of pertinent details can vanish when you get home). Labeling is really important for understanding the history of your rose—you can even tuck a scrap of paper into each plastic bag if that's all you have to write on in an emergency.

My cutting kit, which lives behind the seat of my truck, contains pruning shears, paper towels, baggies, waterproof marking pens, twist-ties (for keeping several cuttings of one variety together), tongue depressors (for writing labels to drop in bags), and some aluminum twist-on tags with a pencil to write on them. When traveling any distance I'm also likely to have a bucket and a cooler with me. The cooler is to keep plant material fresh for a longer time—put a layer of newspaper on top of the ice to protect cuttings from freezer burn. The bucket can be used for rooted suckers some kind gardener may offer to share. (It never hurts to have your own shovel on hand.) Good gardeners tend to be serious thieves—there's even a tradition that says new plants won't grow if you thank the giver instead of pretending you stole them. Tradition aside, however, cuttings must never be taken from private property without full permission, and you must never damage or disfigure a plant from which you are collecting.

Once you've taken the cuttings, which is the easy part, you're up against trying to get them to root. Roses in general root very easily—though this isn't true of every cultivar or of roses in every season. Chinas, Teas, Polyanthas, and Miniatures are known for willingness to set new roots, while iest way to deal with them, if you aren't set up to keep them on agar in petri dishes, is to lay them out on a moist paper towel in a ziplocked plastic bag. You can also put them into jars on top of a lightly moistened layer of fine sphagnum moss. Then put them in the refrigerator and check on them periodically to make sure they're still moist. If they grow a little fungus it's not a disaster, as that may even help break through the seed coat, but they're best kept fairly clean because the fungus can hurt the seedlings if any emerge. Roses can take anywhere from eight weeks to several years to germinate, so patience is the ultimate requirement. Make *sure* you label each batch carefully with the dates and any information about the parentage, because it's hard to remember as time passes.

My best success to date has been with seeds collected from various Hybrid Rugosas, especially *R. rugosa rubra* and 'Hansa'. They grew tiny white root hairs on their paper towel at the end of only nine weeks and were duly transferred to fine damp soil in two-inch pots and kept in bright shade until they adjusted to life in the open. They were moved up to regular potting soil and finally out into the garden as they developed into solid plants—all different, some with pretty flowers, some with mostly blackspot. At the opposite end of the scale are my *Rosa canina* seeds collected by a friend from an abandoned castle garden in Austria. They've been sulking in the fridge for almost a year now, and I don't know if they'll ever give in and sprout. Fortunately there's plenty of room and I don't really have to use the meat drawer (where I keep them) for meat—that can go on another shelf. The obstinacy required to wait them out will make the final plants —if any—even more cherished.

PLANTING ROSES

Planting roses is mainly about dealing with their roots. The roots are the support system for the entire plant and they are what you paid your money for, so don't take them lightly. Assuming that your beds and your plants are all previously prepared, you dig a hole that will allow the roots to spread outward and angle at least a little downward from the crown of the plant. This often means making a small pile of soil in the center of the hole that will hold the crown higher than its appendages. How wide and deep to make the hole depends on the size of the root system, and that is dependent in turn upon whether you're dealing with a hefty grafted rootstock or the fibrous mat of a container-grown plant, or the few long strings on the bottom of your home-propagated cutting. To be safe, work the soil wider and deeper than you think you'll need, and that way you don't risk committing the cardinal sins of crowding the roots or squashing them in with the ends bent upwards. Roots are supposed to grow out and down, and that's what they're going to do, so incorrect planting means they'll take a while to sort themselves out and spread, which is time wasted that could be spent on blooming.

Some gardeners like to work a little fertilizer into the hole when planting. It's not really necessary to fertilize until the roses have settled in and started to grow; in fact, you don't want to stimulate them too much until the root system is stable in its new conditions. Also, certain fertilizers can burn the roots and reduce the plant's vigor. If inviting a new friend to the garden without providing some kind of edible entertainment makes you feel like a bad hostess, stick to slow-release organics like sea weed and alfalfa that will promote new basal breaks and strong growth. You can also work a cup of finished compost into the hole before you add the rose. That way you won't burn it or push it too hard, but you'll be helping it build up vigor and health.

Once you have the hole prepared, it's time to put the rose in it. This is the time to clean up your mail-order plants, if you haven't already done so. I remember the first time I was sent into the garden with some containerized roses and a shovel. I had never gardened before in my life, though already a woman grown, and I experienced a flickering moment of doubt about whether or not to remove the roses from the pots before planting them. I would absolutely *never* confess to this, except that more than one novice gardener has come to me with the same question. The answer is yes, you do take them out of the pots unless (see container planting section) there are very special circumstances. If they are soaking in a bucket, take them out of the bucket. Only the rose and whatever soil is part of its root ball go in the ground.

If the rose is bare root, settle the crown on top of the mound of soil in the hole, spread the roots comfortably around it and fill the hole back in. If it was container grown, turn it upside down, support the crown with one hand and slide the pot off with the other. Then use both hands to set the soil and root mass as one unit into the hole and work the soil back firmly around the edges with fingers or shovel. In this latter case you don't need to worry about a central soil mound or messing with the roots at all unless the plant is rootbound. If the roots are very large and have begun wrapping in circles around the inside of the pot, they should be spread out as much as possible so they'll grow correctly when planted. Sometime roses are purchased bare root by a nursery and then potted up and sold in containers, to expand the season of availability. If you get one that's just been potted, all the dirt will promptly fall off when you tip it out. Treat if just like a bare root rose and it will be fine. Others may be transplanted into pressed peat pots, and if left too long their roots will grow into the walls of the pot. You can't take these plants out of the container without injuring the tiny feeder roots, but you can slit the sides of the pot in several places, or clip through it with your

MAINTAINING THE ROSES

When roses have been installed in their prepared beds or containers and are more or less established, the long-term tasks of rose gardening begin. These necessary chores make up most of a gardener's interaction with the living plants, and they include weeding, watering, feeding, and grooming—which covers pruning all roses and the training of climbing varieties—with the awareness of certain seasonal requirements. Searching for signs of trouble—usually pests and diseases—is also part of gardening, but most aspects of troubleshooting are dealt with in the next chapter. Regular maintenance chores are the equivalent of feeding, watering, and brushing your dog—as opposed to checking him for tapeworm and taking him to the vet for vaccinations. These tasks are homey, friendly things that are the basis of the pleasurable bond most gardeners establish with their gardens.

WEEDING

Weeding is a task that gets a lot of bad press, but in a well-prepared, well-mulched garden it's really pretty satisfying. You have to get down in the dirt, but most weeds come out fairly easily by hand or with a trowel, and they can go straight into the compost pile or to the chickens, so it's not unlike harvesting vegetables—radishes or carrots, perhaps. Also, weeding diminishes as the bed becomes established, unless you make the mistake of adding uncomposted cow manure full of pasture seeds or mulching with hay rather than straw. Even really irritating weeds like nut grass are easier to discourage when the soil itself is properly maintained.

A big question in any garden is which are the "weeds" and which are the "flowers." In a rose garden I feel that anything threatening the well-being of the roses is automatically a weed. Roses are fine about sharing space with a diversity of other plants, but they can't take being completely smothered and having their light and air supply cut off. It doesn't matter whether the aggressor is an outsider, or a deliberately chosen garden plant. I let a gorgeous Turk's cap mallow expand to its largest dimensions one year, and was extremely distressed when I suddenly remembered a planting of the Miniature 'Rise 'n' Shine' had been put in as a bright accent when the mallow was small. After searching through the foliage for a while I found the little roses—all stiff and brown—and I've felt ever since that Turk's cap is basically a weed. The point is to keep your beds in balance, by removing anything that's inappropriately sized or too greedy of the essentials all the plants need to share. And remember, nothing can replace the daily attention of the gardener in keeping weeds manageable and the garden at its best.

Anytime you weed, you leave pockets of air in the soil where the weed roots were lodged. Pulling the weeds out is a good way to keep the soil loose and nicely cultivated, but it's important to protect the roots of the other plants in the beds by watering immediately afterwards. This is particularly critical in hot weather, when weeding without watering can cause serious stress damage.

A final tip on weeding is to protect your roses at all times from that useful invention, the weedeater. Roses planted in public areas and as specimen plants in lawns or along fence lines are especially at risk of being damaged or killed by girdling from the whirling nylon cutting cord. Even if you can't make a protective bed for every plant, consider mulching under them with thick straw or anything that will smother weeds and thus keep the maintenance crew at a safe distance.

*W*ATERING

Many roses are fairly drought tolerant (and neglect tolerant!), but there's no denying they'll perform better and stay healthier with regular watering. Rain water is best, because it lacks hardening minerals and contains some nitrogen (from the electrical activity of lightning), but roses like plenty of any kind of water, about an inch a week to thoroughly soak their roots. They don't, with the exception of the Swamp Rose (*R. palustris*), appreciate constantly wet feet. They also like water above and below their foliage to blast off pests such as aphids and spider mites and powdery mildew spores, but they don't do well with leaves that stay wet overnight and let the soil above the roots just before seasonal mulching, and everything else is pretty much gravy. The microbes in the compost will help process and break down existing nutrients so that plant roots can use them, and the organic material supplies further nutrients and improves general soil structure.

There's no denying, however, the satisfaction that comes from pumping a bush up a little and getting it to bloom at its personal best. Just remember that too much nitrogen (usually from overenthusiastic foliar feeding) can stimulate too much new growth, which attracts certain pests—too much of any one element can cause a problem of some kind. Before you add anything other than compost, you really should do a soil test and find out where you stand. You'll rarely stay too high in nitrogen because it breaks down so quickly, but in heavy soils it's easy to build up an overload of lingering phosphorus from bone meal or colloidal phosphate. The result can be a chlorosis that mimics nitrogen deficiency, when the real trouble is nutrients being locked up by the soil imbalance. If you do the soil tests, you won't have to waste time guessing. Also, you'll want to give the heaviest feedings in spring and fall, when the work of blooming will be burning up the nutrients, with lighter feedings in the heat of summer and very little nitrogen before the new-growth-killing frosts of winter. Obviously, it's most sensible to use small, frequent portions of low potency fertilizers (liquid solutions of fish emulsion, or manure or compost tea, sprayed on the leaves early in the morning, are great for this) or seasonal additions of slow-release mixtures adjusted to your own soil conditions. Be moderate in your nurturing unless you're the kind of person who likes to sit in the garden with *The Compendium of Rose Diseases*, trying to match the blotches on each leaf to color plates of a specific mineral excess or deficiency. As with any fertilizers, try to water the roses thoroughly both before and after applications to make sure their roots will be able to take in the nutrients you're trying to give them.

In addition to the compost I like to give my roses some alfalfa, soybean, and/or seaweed three or four times a year, with bone meal before the spring and fall bloom (phosphorus doesn't build up in my sandy soil), and supplemental feedings of diluted fish emulsion to keep soil nitrogen levels fairly constant as my mulch decomposes. (The fish emulsion may be applied as a drench or foliar spray, depending on whether I happen across the sprayer or the bucket first.) Gardeners are very like cooks: everyone wants to adjust the recipes a little to suit their own tastes, and this is actually good because every gardener is working in a private micro-ecology of their own. The following fertilizers are all useful, and you can work out your own blend, with the results of your soil test and information from other gardeners in your local area in mind. Be aware that if you are using or selling your roses as food, you'll need to check with your local organic certification agency to be sure that each amendment or fertilizer is listed specifically for use on "Herbs." Roses aren't yet listed as an agricultural food crop. And always follow any label directions that a product may offer.

$\mathcal{Q}$UICK REFERENCE

FOR NITROGEN (N): alfalfa, blood meal, fish emulsion and fish meal, guano (highly variable), compost (variable), seaweed and kelp (low), manures (cow is usually lowest), soybean meal.

FOR PHOSPHORUS (P): bone meal, colloidal phosphate, compost, guano, manure (low).

FOR POTASSIUM (K): alfalfa, compost, fish, granite dust, greensand, kelp, manure (low), soybean meal.

$\mathcal{C}$OMMON ORGANIC FERTILIZERS

ALFALFA: One of the all-time best ingredients in rose foods, alfalfa has moderate levels of the three main nutrients (5%N–1%P–2%K), plus a natural growth stimulant—the fatty acid triaconatol, plus some trace minerals. Half a cup twice a year lightly worked into the soil around the bush is about right for the dry pellets or meal. It can also be used as a "pick-me-up" infusion, made by soaking about a cup of pellets in five gallons of water for several days, then pouring on one gallon per bush.

BLOOD MEAL: High in nitrogen (10 to 15%N–0 to 3%P–0%K) and often in price. It works quickly, but can burn roots if overapplied. Blood meal is frequently obtained from the process of purifying bone meal. Agricultural bone meal from the feed store, with a yellowish greasy look, often still has the blood meal in it and is a much cheaper and better product than the little bags of either one sold by nurseries. A few tablespoons per bush at the start of each growing season (spring and fall), well watered-in, should be enough.

BONE MEAL: High in phosphorus (up to 4%N–11 to 34%P—0%K), it also has a lot of calcium (up to 30%) and helps roses root and bloom just as well as bulbs. Bone meal breaks down slowly over about six months. Since it raises the soil pH, make sure you need the phosphorus before you apply this. See note on blood meal for the best source for this. A half cup per bush, twice a year, is enough.

COLLOIDAL PHOSPHATE: Another high phosphorus product (0%N–14 to 20%P–0%K) with about 20% calcium, plus iron, high silica, and some trace minerals. An excellent product for phosphate-starved soils, as it breaks down slowly over a two- or three-year period. It also raises the soil pH, so once again, be sure you need it before you use it. Rock phosphate has the same basic properties but is a mined, non-renewable resource. Use one half cup of colloidal phosphate per bush every two years, or five pounds per one hundred square feet during bed preparation.

COMPOST: Slightly acidic, slow-acting, and well-balanced (½ % to 4%

of N, P, and K), compost also improves soil quality. Easy to make at home, though it can sometimes be purchased (for a high price) at nurseries that carry mulches and other soil amendments. You probably can't add too much, but a few cups per bush worked into the soil four times a year, then covered with protective mulch, should keep the roses fairly happy.

EPSOM SALTS: One of the few elements not found in nature that the National Organic Board has on its approval list. Epsom salts is magnesium sulfate, at 9.8% magnesium and 6% sulfur, and roses really like this combination in small doses. It helps promote root growth, basal breaks, strong canes, lush foliage, and shapely flowers—though alfalfa may be nearly as effective. Epsom salts dissolves easily and absorbs quickly, but don't get carried away and overapply. Magnesium sulfate leaches very slowly from the soil, and an excess can be toxic to roses. Consider getting a soil test before using Epsom salts—some California soils are already quite high in magnesium. If your soil can really use it, twice a year is plenty, at the rate of two or three tablespoons per bush at spring pruning and the same about a month after the fall pruning.

FISH EMULSION: A nice, moderately balanced (4%N–1 to 4%P–2%K) fertilizer that can be used as a foliar spray for quick feeding or a root drench at regular intervals. Follow directions on the bottle for correct mixing. Most fish emulsion is sold "deodorized" but don't let that fool you; it can smell pretty strong for a few days after application. Fish emulsion also has a little sulfur in it, which may help with controlling fungal diseases. Fish meal is available as well, has higher nitrogen levels, and breaks down more slowly—if you use it, apply about one pound per rose bush once a year.

GRANITE DUST: A good source of potassium (0%N–0%P–3 to 5%K) with 67% silica and a lot of trace minerals. Granite dust has been the guilt-free answer to greensand for a number of years. Apply it when preparing the bed at the rate of ten pounds per one hundred square feet, or as part of a fertilizer mix worked into the soil at about one pound per rose bush. It lasts up to ten years, so it doesn't need to be included often unless soil tests show a potassium deficiency.

GREENSAND: An excellent product with a bad reputation—for a while the only source was strip mining. Check with your supplier to clear your conscience before buying. Greensand has negligible amounts of nitrogen and phosphorus, but about 6% potassium, 50% silica, roughly 20% iron, and thirty-two trace minerals. The result is a slightly acidic soil loosener with a long lifespan. Work it into the initial bed preparation at the rate of between five and ten pounds per one hundred square feet, then forget about it for ten years.

GUANO: A time-honored fertilizer, sea bird guano was all the rage during the nineteenth century. Today we're more likely to see bat guano—hopefully mined from caves when the bats are away on migration. Either product is useful and generally higher than other manures in nutrients and trace minerals, though different sources vary widely (1 to 14%N–4 to 15%P–0 to 3%K). Read the bags carefully to see what you're getting. Guano, also like other manures, is a good general soil amendment, but the price is often prohibitively high. Add the amount you can afford, adjusted by the requirements of your soil tests and the levels listed on that particular bag.

GYPSUM: Gypsum is calcium sulfate, with between 23 and 57% calcium and about 17% sulfur. It has a neutral pH, so it shouldn't affect the balance of your soil adversely and may even help severely alkaline soils. It slowly acts to make clay soils crumbly, so that roots can penetrate better and drainage is improved. It also helps leach salts if you have salty water problems. Gypsum functions best when worked into the bed during the initial preparation, at a rate of about four pounds per one hundred square feet. It can be added later, worked into the surface of the soil as well as possible, at about one half cup per rose bush. Environmental activists recommend using only gypsum from mined sources.

MANURE: Manures vary in nutrient content depending upon their age and the dietary habits of the source animal. The commonly available kinds run about 4%N–2%P–2%K, with cow being the lowest at about half that. Some zoo and circus animal manures may be higher. Manure is best used well composted or aged to prevent burning the plant roots, and is considered a soil amendment with slow-release nutrients included. At this time sludge products from city waste water systems are not listed as "manure" but as synthetic products because of contents such as residue from household cleaners, so they are not included in this category. Application rates of animal manures depend on how much you have available; like any composted organic material, it's hard to add too much. Three to five pounds per bush once or twice a year will be very useful.

SEAWEED: Sold variously as kelp meal, kelp, seaweed extract, or liquid seaweed, all these excellent products have about the same nutrient balance (1 to 3%N–0%P–1 to 3%K). They also contain wonderful trace minerals, growth hormones, micronutrients, amino acids, and vitamins. The meals and extracts can be added to the soil as per manufacturers' directions once or twice a year and will help feed the vital microbes around the roots. Liquid seaweed can be also used, well-diluted, as a foliar spray to help boost an ailing plant or treat transplant shock. Some brands are very oily and can leave a residue on the foliage that will burn in the sun, so try each one before treating the whole garden.

SOYBEAN MEAL: This amendment is a useful source of nitrogen and potassium (7%N–½%P–2%K) and helps feed soil microbes, so it's a good addition to a compost application. It's a soy industry byproduct that it used for animal food and can usually be found in feed stores. Use roughly one cup per rose bush two to four times per year.

SULFUR: This will lower the soil pH if you have trouble with alkalinity,

Bushy Roses

Roses that form upright bushes can come in any size. Most Miniatures, Polyanthas, Floribundas, and Hybrid Teas fall into this group, as do a majority of Hybrid Rugosas. Most of the roses lumped into the Shrub class are of this type. Among the older roses, Chinas, Teas, and a number of Bourbons offer a wide choice of varieties that grow into fat bushes. Even the very old European roses, such as Gallicas and Damasks, include some thick bushes in their numbers. The bushy shrubs are great for hedging, edging, and container growing as well as for filling in spaces in any flower bed.

Everyone has heard, by now, of pruning bush roses with hedge shears or even a chainsaw. Interestingly enough this approach works just fine. Any scars left behind by rough clipping are soon hidden from view by new growth and forgotten. When a bush can measure six feet across in every direction, pruning with hedge shears is a very time-saving solution. It's also addictive to some gardeners. There's a certain sense of loss that those of us with lots of roses experience when we've zoomed through bush after bush and suddenly reach the end, with nothing left to attack and subdue. The problem with rough clipping, however, is that over time it allows the build-up of dead twigs and crowded, spindly shoots in the interior of the plant. If you use the hedge shears to cut back an established bush by approximately one third of its total mass, you have the worst of the chore out of the way in no time at all. Then you can go back and clear out the small stuff with sharp hand clippers, grooming the plant properly for a healthy bloom season. Most garden roses need no more severe pruning than this, and some will actively protest a hard pruning (more than one half the length of the canes) by withholding flowers until they've grown back to a comfortable size.

Arching Roses

A number of roses, particularly among the Hybrid Musk, Centifolia, Alba, and Species classes, have bushes whose canes curve gracefully up and over towards the ground. This is a lovely effect, making a cascade of flowers when they're in full bloom. Arching shrubs can be used as specimen plants, standing alone in the lawn or along the fence. Their flowing branches also make a good backdrop to enhance water features. Some, such as the Polyantha variety 'The Fairy', are small enough to grow gracefully in containers on a patio. Others, like the Species *Rosa palustris*, the Swamp Rose, can eventually get head high and spread wider than you can reach. In order to encourage the natural form, I prefer not to cut back the canes at all, but to just thin their number as necessary, removing any angular, dead, or unsightly growth in the process. Cuts should be made neatly, removing rejected canes close to their point of branching without leaving ugly stubs. Stubs produce new little growth breaks, like witch fingers, at their ends. This is great for bushy shrubs where multiple branching fills out the form, but it spoils the graceful lines of an arching rose.

CLIMBING ROSES

As with arching roses, the natural form of a climber is part of its beauty, so the long canes shouldn't be shortened or cut back. Vigorous climbers need to be retrained or to have loose ends tucked in at least once a year, and preferably more often if they have a long growing season. At the time you train them you can remove any dead canes, thinning the total to a manageable number and cutting off whatever you don't like. Once again, cuts should be made cleanly and close to the point of branching, or all the way down at the base.

TRAINING CLIMBERS

The canes that you keep can be trained in a number of ways, wrapped or braided around a post, fanned out, or woven on a trellis. Just make sure that they don't go straight up, or all the flowers will be out of reach at the very top. Training the canes away from the vertical breaks the flow of nutrients to the tip and promotes leafy growth and flowers all along the cane. It also allows for nearly unlimited creativity in using climbing roses as decorations for all parts of the house and garden.

Roses can catch hold with their prickles in something like a tree crotch, but they have no equipment for clinging to walls, posts, or trellises. In working with climbing roses you'll need a roll of jute twine or other soft tie material to gently fasten the growing canes to the supports of your choice. Jute is an organic fiber easy to get at the hardware store or nursery and flexible enough to let canes expand with growth, plus it's biodegradable. Stretch tie is also useful, but it looks like and is plastic, and you end up with bright green tags of it here and there in the garden. Jute vanishes into the soil, improving tilth, no doubt, as it disintegrates. I usually add a hammer (well-made pruning shears can tolerate a fair amount of nail and staple pounding, but I'm sure this is wrong) to my training kit, and a small paper bag with a supply of fencing staples—the staples I placed last time are somehow in completely inconvenient places next time I want to use them. Using staples or nails as fastening points allows more precise arrangement of the canes and thus requires less tie material, which is both more economical and shows up less in the finished result.

When attaching rose canes, don't bind them so tightly that they'll get

LEFT: Weaving 'American Beauty, Cl.' on a pillar. RIGHT: Using stretch tie to train a climber—although jute is better in the organic rose garden.

choked off as they grow. Overly loose fastenings, on the other hand, allow the rose canes to move with the wind and get wounded by chafing. This can lead to canker and insect infestations, or broken canes. If you can't easily judge how tight to fasten, consider making a figure-eight tie so that the rose is protected by a twist of twine from the hard metal or wood.

TRAINING PEGGED ROSES

Pegged roses are hard to categorize as they are treated very much like climbers, but they are usually shorter, with canes in the five- to seven-foot range. Most of these varieties are normally pruned as bushy shrubs, but will throw out long canes that don't quite fit the form. They can be trained as short pillar roses, but pegging such a rose is a way to turn an awkwardly lanky bush into an interesting arching shrub by pruning it like a climber, then curving the canes down to the garden bed and fastening them there with long hooks or staples (at least eight inches to hold well in good soil) made of wire. You can bend your own out of old coat hangers, or purchase non-rusting commercial pegging hooks. When pressed into the soil, it's hard to tell whether you got the pricey ones or not. Drawbacks to this method are the long canes that sprout each season and can't be fastened down until they've lost the first brittle succulence of new growth, and the tendency of pegged canes to take root at the tips as if they were intentionally layered.

Choosing how high or low to arch the canes is dependent upon the flexibility of the plant—'Madame Isaac Pereire' is one of the all-time great roses for this—and your own taste. If you can get a pegged rose to look like anything except a handsomely large spider when not in bloom, you'll have made a breakthrough in design. It is possible, of course, to train these same types of roses along a low wire fence—maybe two feet high—and create a long flowering border for the front of a bed, or to fasten artistic weights to the ends of the canes so that they arch over but don't touch the ground. True pegging, however, is about arranging spiders in your garden and enjoying their masses of flowers when in bloom. That's the time when you forget about the grooming problems and just delight in the results.

GENERAL PRUNING TIPS

An important question in pruning is whether or not diseases can be transmitted from plant to plant through the wounds made by the clippers. In a very few cases, such as with crown gall, this is a real possibility. Most common rose diseases, however, will not be carried to another plant by the pruning shears. If you have recently received roses from unknown sources and have concerns about their health, prune them as a group and then sterilize the clippers in something like alcohol or hydrogen peroxide before rinsing them off and doing the rest of the garden. Otherwise, sterilization of pruning tools will probably not be necessary in ordinary gardening.

A second common concern is about precision pruning. Gardeners new to roses conscientiously read through the literature and agonize about cutting back each cane to a precise length at an exact angle with an outward facing axillary bud. In pruning garden roses the amount to cut back is really up to you, though most shrubs don't need to be trimmed by more than one third to one half the length of each cane, and less is just fine. Some huge specimen roses seem to thrive with almost no cutting back at all, and the more bush you leave, within the limits of grooming for health and form, the more area will be covered with flowers. As for the angle of the cut, this is more critical on varieties whose canes tend to die back at the ends if not carefully slanted to shed moisture, like Hybrid Perpetuals and Hybrid Teas. Twiggy, rapidly growing roses such as China, Tea, or Polyantha varieties are hardly affected at all by dieback. Cutting at an angle is thus a good habit to develop, but not a desperate necessity in most cases. The same is true of trying to choose an outward-facing bud. While this is probably helpful for broadening rose bushes that grow stiffly erect, like Hybrid Teas, it isn't critical for most well-branched varieties. The direction of the axillary bud (found at the junction of leaf and cane) signals the direction that the new cane break will grow—if it doesn't do something else instead under the influence of various genetic and environmental factors. Since not all classes of roses have as few or as stiff canes as do most Hybrid Teas, there is really no comprehensive rule for where to point each bud when you are simply pruning for health and beauty in the garden.

*W*HEN TO PRUNE

In cold zones pruning is a once-a-year task to perform in the early spring, about three to four weeks before the last average frost. The minor chore of tidying up the roses in the late fall after they're dormant, to prevent winter wind damage, shouldn't be approached as real pruning. That chore should take place just before the roses break dormancy again, to ensure that none of that massive surge of spring energy is wasted on material that will have to be cut off. Where I garden, in zone 8, knowledgeable gardeners prune twice a year, repeating the process with a less intensive clipping in the late summer (three or four weeks before the hot weather usually breaks) to take advantage of our spectacular fall bloom season.

Not only do these pruning times work with the weather to promote the strongest, healthiest roses, but most roses can be relied upon to reach a peak of bloom six or seven weeks after pruning. With this information you can more or less time the flowers to be at their best for a specific event, such as a garden party or wedding. The knowledge is also useful if you plan to exhibit your roses on a specific date. The majority of roses will also tolerate a little light trimming, or dead-heading, after each flush of bloom, and this encourages them to immediately focus on blooming again. Dead-heading between heavy pruning sessions is not critical for the health or well-being of garden roses, but it does keep them looking tidy and may increase the blooming a little. Remontant (repeat-blooming) roses form their flowers on new growth, so the more they are stimulated to grow the more flowers they can produce.

The exception to this rule, and this is important, is roses that only bloom once each year. These spring bloomers produce flowers on old wood rather than new, i.e., canes that have hardened over a winter. Because of this they only should be pruned between one and three months *after* blooming. If you clip them in the spring before they bloom, you'll cut away half the flowers.

There are two times to consider *not* dead-heading your remontant roses, even if you prefer a tidy appearance. The first is in the summer, in the South, when temperatures that stay in the high 80's or low 90's even at night will create a kind of heat dormancy. If you push the roses to grow and bloom during this time, you'll have to be prepared to offer them extra water and you'll still see smaller and fewer flowers than in fall and spring. The second time to hold back the clippers is in the middle of autumn. If you've pruned for the fall bloom and had a good display, you may want to leave the roses alone after that. In a long growing season they can probably be pushed to one more serious effort, but you run the risk of a frost catching them with all their resources exposed in the fragile new growth. Besides, if you trim them all the time, you'll never know which varieties might have made hips. Hips, the fruits of the rose, are a visually interesting feature in the garden and also can be made into tasty jams, tarts, and soups full of vitamin C (see chapter 9).

A final caution about pruning is that very young bushes need a little time to grow before they get cut back a lot. If you're planting bare-root roses, by all means clean them up and get their shape balanced when you put them in the ground. Even container-grown plants can often use a little grooming to get them growing in the right direction after they've been crowded together in the field. After that, skip a pruning season to let them fill out and you'll soon get larger plants that can really benefit from being properly cut.

Rosa wichuraiana hips, a late season bonus.

$\int$EASONAL CARE

Most rose books explain how to prepare for long bouts of freezing weather, but no one ever mentions the heat. In the South we contend with the latter much more often than the former, and gardeners need to prepare for that as well—or even instead. We have two intense bloom seasons, spring and fall, and they're divided by two periods of more or less dormant behavior. Winter dormancy consists of shedding foliage, stopping bloom and storing the majority of the plant's energy in the soil-protected roots—unless it's so mild out that the roses try to keep going all season. Since this leaves the plants more vulnerable to our sudden freezes, it's not great—but you can't really talk a rose into going winter dormant just because you know it should (roses need to be pruned whether they go fully dormant or not). Summer dormancy often means shedding some foliage as well, or having foliage so heat-stressed that blackspot takes it off. Flowers are still produced, but not in quantity and rarely of normal size and color. You should neither choose nor reject a rose based on what it manages to display in July and August; remember, you don't really want to be out in the garden then, either.

In addition to adjusting pruning practices so you don't stimulate new growth in excessively hot or cold weather, there are some other ways to keep roses comfortable and healthy through these times of stress. First of all, never let them get desperate for water if the thermometer is at one extreme or the other—above 85° or below 20°. Keeping the soil cool and moist in the summer helps roses be at their best when they reach fall blooming season. Winter watering acts as a layer of insulation—water holds heat much better than soil—and combats the effects of cold dry winds. Second, of course, is mulching to protect the soil's moisture. A good blanket of mulch acts as insulation and also as a barrier between the rose and fungus spores resting in the soil. Applying it when the seasons change will keep the roses stronger and healthier. Before applying the mulch, consider scratching a handful of compost into the soil for each rose. Compost has nutrients that are slowly released, maintaining overall health without pushing a plant to perform when it should be resting. Cutting back on nitrogen fertilizer, in particular, before a tough season will help a rose reach a stable state of dormancy (in winter) or semi-dormancy (in summer) so that growth slows down and plant's life force is conserved for better times.

Studying your roses in winter is almost as important as nurturing them at that season; their dormant appearance may help you decide how best to use them in the garden. Some roses go through an awkward state with half their foliage on and half off, others remain gloriously leafy, and some that go completely dormant reveal hidden beauties to be treasured. The Hybrid Alba 'Madame Plantier' is one of these, with its fountain of silvery canes. Roses that turn color, like the Gallica 'La Belle Sultane', whose rusty orange autumn leaves drop to reveal a cluster

'La Belle Sultane' in winter—the burgundy canes make a nice backdrop to the golden daffodils.

'Madame Plantier's' amazing grace in winter.

of burgundy whips, are extremely interesting in the fall and winter garden. Climbing roses can also show to advantage when the spare lines of their bare forms are exposed. You can expect a healthy rose to be with you a long time, through all kinds of weather, so learning about its seasonal needs and talents is definitely of value.

TROUBLE-SHOOTING

The idea of organic rose gardening is to minimize the amount of detailed technical maintenance you have to do by working sensibly to keep the soil and surrounding environment healthy. Since we ultimately control neither Mother Nature nor the choices of our neighbors, there will still be some occasions when you have to take action against specific garden problems. Pests and diseases can come in from outside your garden any time, carried in on infected material, borne in on the breezes, or motoring along under their own power. To minimize their damaging potential and improve the overall health of your property, there are a number of possibilities to consider. The very last choice of any practical gardener is to resort to chemical attack that can unbalance the ecology of the entire area. Here are some alternative methods of expanding your rose garden's ability to take care of itself.

1. DIVERSIFICATION. Be creative in designing with roses, and don't make a garden with nothing but roses in it. This is like ringing a dinner bell for the pests that specialize in attacking them. With a mixture of healthy plants, mixed information is broadcast into the atmosphere. Also, physical barriers break up the pathogen pathways between roses, so a number of insects and diseases can thus be avoided. Try using roses from all different classes, as they have varied natural susceptibility to specific types of problems. Include some of the wilder roses, if you have space, letting big climbers and shrubs naturalize to provide havens for insect-eating birds as part of a complete ecosystem.

2. COMPANION PLANTING/PLANT GUILDS. Certain plants have an apparent deterrent effect on specific pests and diseases, though not all of them that gardeners recommend have been thoroughly researched and doc-

LEFT: A beneficial lizard bug hunting.
BELOW: 'Nearly Wild' interplanted with artemisia.

umented. Other plants are considered to promote the health and vigor of those around them. Once established in your garden as permanent plant guilds, these friendly neighbors may make a real difference to the overall health of the roses. Companion plants suggested for the rose garden include alliums (the whole garlic and onion family), catnip, thyme, rosemary, artemisias (not *A. absinthium*—it's strongly allelopathic and prevents other plants from growing nearby—but gentler forms such as southernwood), alyssum, tansy, coriander, fennel, nasturtiums, petunias, mint, and geraniums. Try growing combinations of these, especially the first six, very close around susceptible roses. The alliums (my favorites are elephant garlic,

'Lichterloh' with society garlic.

leeks, and their cousin, society garlic), which can be grown right through a rose bush, are most important; they even help a little with fungal diseases if left in the same location for several years. Invasive companion plants such as tansy and mint can be grown in containers within the garden, or sunk into the soil in bottomless pots. Through your own experimentation you can find great combinations in which all the plants thrive, beneficial insects are attracted, and the bad bugs mostly stay away. These cooperative plant guilds can be established throughout your landscape as well as within the garden proper.

3. BENEFICIAL INSECTS. These predators of pest insects are fun, functional, and educational. Most suppliers can give you information on suitable varieties and how to get them established. Make sure you ask, because different species need different handling to work for you in the garden. For general first-time use, try lacewing larvae—they're voracious! Or raise ladybeetle nymphs. These odd-looking larvae eat more aphids than the adults (which often fly off unless locally purchased after laying their eggs). Praying mantises, also called devil horses, are highly entertaining as they stalk through foliage like Godzilla on a rampage in Tokyo. As you learn the quirks of various beneficial insects and release more into your garden, you'll be re-establishing healthy, balanced populations within your whole neighborhood. Try to discourage your neighbors from using pesticides that will kill your new pets. Chip in together for Trichogramma wasps and make the release a community event. Get kids who have to do biology projects to figure out what the most common local garden pests are and what beneficial predator will best control them. And don't forget to honor your existing garden helpers. Lizards, spiders, bees, birds, and earthworms are likely to be in your garden already, and they're all extremely valuable for the roles they play in the natural cycle.

4. NECTARY AND SHELTER PLANTS. Your beneficial insects need certain kinds of plants for shelter and food between waves of pests. If you don't have a nice weedy area close to your garden and don't, for some reason, want to plant a weed belt around your garden, there are still several options. Consider working with your neighborhood association to turn any vacant lots into attractive wildflower plantings, encouraging a healthy balance of insect life in the immediate area. Everybody's garden will benefit from the result. Within your own garden, include tansy, dill, fennel, catnip, yarrow, butterfly weed (*Asclepias tuberosa*), coreopsis, gaillardia, asters, marigolds, and even a few goldenrod plants. The more invasive of these (tansy, yarrow, goldenrod) can be kept under control by planting them in bottomless pots, to keep the roots from spreading. All of them are attractive to one or more beneficial insects.

5. HEDGEROWS AND BARRIERS. A windbreak of some kind will keep a number of bugs out of your garden. Lightly motivated or low-flying varieties are deterred by a physical barrier close to the plants of their choice. Take your whole property into consideration on this: why plant in the center of the yard, when you can make your privacy fence work to shelter your garden? Does the wall of your house block the prevailing wind? Maybe if you incorporate that shed to form one side, with a row of sunflowers on the other? Just remember that the plants within the barriers will still need light and air.

BELOW: Lady beetle nymphs protecting a rose. BELOW RIGHT: 'Mermaid' bloom and bee.

6. QUARANTINE. If you get roses from an unknown source, or from a known source of disease or pest problems, keep them growing

in a container in an area away from the rest of your garden for a period of one to two years, or until you can be sure that they're clean. Avoiding the introduction of diseased or infested material into your garden means avoiding the work it would take to clean everything up again—a year's quarantine will seem like nothing in comparison. If you have serious concerns about a new rose, you can wash it off in mild soapy water, roots and all, and repot it in clean soil. It will still need quarantine, but it will stand a better chance of recovery. Check with your local organic certifiers or agricultural extension agent to find out the period of quarantine recommended for any imported roses.

  7. **LAWN AND HOUSE CARE.** Treat these areas as carefully as you treat your rose garden. Chemical fertilizers and pesticides used near the garden will still affect the garden. Consider developing a less than one hundred percent grass lawn and including short clovers to attract beneficial insects, or using native grasses (like buffalo) that require less chemical support. Treat for fleas and fire ants as suggested in the following pest control list. As a tip, keep turf grass from surrounding your trees—it has an allelopathic (toxic) affect on their health. Try underplanting instead with native shrubs or shade tolerant mints, or even using liriope as a border to keep the grass well away from the trunk. Healthy trees will attract fewer pests to your yard.

  8. **ALTERNATIVE SPRAYS.** If you must spray something, be gentle. Foliar feeding with compost tea, alfalfa, or fish emulsion and seaweed, will give the roses a vitality boost that may help them throw off a pest or disease problem on their own. A simple hard water spray that washes above and below the leaves can knock off a lot of pests and even powdery mildew spores. Try the baking soda solution for general fungus diseases (1 tablespoon baking soda and 1 tablespoon lightweight horticultural oil to 1 gallon of water), applied late in the evening or very early in the morning, the day after a thorough watering—the foliage needs to be dry so direct sun won't burn it. If you use this mild spray for fungus diseases, make sure that you do so on a regular basis: haphazard applications don't seem to produce reliable results. Sulfur spray is also effective for fungus, long-lasting on the foliage (it leaves a slight, grayish residue), and safe to use, though much smellier than the baking soda. The rotten egg scent dissipates, fortunately, as the spray dries. Safer™ makes a commercial fungicide that uses sulfur as the active ingredient and is properly labeled for rose use. For insect problems, Safer™ insecticidal soaps labeled for roses are very effective for knocking back high levels of many pests while waiting for the beneficial insects to arrive. You may want to avoid garlic spray, or use it just for spot treatments—it's safe for humans and helps with fungus, but it's a broad spectrum insecticide that will kill beneficials as well as pests.

  All of the above ingredients, including baking soda and horticultural oil (including all dormant oils), are on the list recommended for approval by the National Organic Standards Program (NOSP) in the near future. To be certain that what you're using is allowed, you must work closely with your own state organic certification agency, particularly if you are or want to be certified as an organic grower. The contact address for finding your state certification agencies is listed in the Resource section. Some of the things that are *not* recommended for the NOSP list at this time are other familiar home-recipe ingredients such as dish soap, Lysol™, and Listerine™. Neem oil as a spray or systemic is also somewhat questionable, though it may eventually be approved by the Environmental Protection Agency in some specific formulations and thus be recommended in those products for the NOSP list. Anti-transpirant sprays such as Wiltpruf™ have been recorded as having fungus control and prevention benefits in addition to their primary function, but they aren't currently even being considered for organic approval. If you aren't certified organic but want to grow as if you were, there's a simple rule of thumb. If all the ingredients in your product of choice are scheduled to be on the NOSP list, it should be morally all right to use even if not listed itself. Be aware that any home concoction will be likely to vary in strength from batch to batch, and that it is illegal to market your private mixture without proper licensing and labeling. To find out more about substances that are listed as approved for organic use, contact your own state's certification agent (see Resources) for further information.

If you do spray, water thoroughly the day before so that the plants are not water-stressed. Then wait until the sun is off the plant in the evening, or do it before the sun is very strong early in the morning. This will allow the foliage to dry and prevent burning by refraction through droplets of moisture. Spraying can be a chore, but it also ensures that you spend quality time with each rose bush and learn more about its individual habits, quirks, and beauties.

9. DEVELOP TOLERANCE. You don't have to know the solution to every rose problem if you can learn to see beauty in good health overall, without demanding total perfection. It's even possible to grow show-quality blooms on a bush that has blackspot on a few leaves. Discovering the difference between a balanced situation and a serious blight will save a lot of stress and give you more time to genuinely appreciate your garden and the world around it.

COMMON ROSE DISEASES AND CONTROLS

BLACKSPOT: Peak development of this fungus is during warm, wet weather. Overwinters in leaf buds, within canes, or on fallen leaves. Black spots appear on the foliage and canes, followed by yellowing and leaf drop. Plenty of sun, good air movement, and healthy soil increase plant resistance. Periodic clean-up of shed leaves, particularly in the late fall after dormancy

Blackspot getting started.

or early spring before the buds begin to swell will limit the number of spores lying around and help prevent overwintering of the disease. These leaves can be fairly safely composted in a hot pile, otherwise they can be burned. After clean-up, apply some compost to increase over-all health and disease resistance, and then put down your mulch. The compost and mulch act as a physical barrier between the plant and any spores in the soil. Allium plants, grown in the same place for three years or more, seem to have some benefit in controlling fungus spores in the soil by exudations of small amounts of sulfur. Spraying the foliage with "compost tea" (live compost soaked in water for several days, at about a one to five ratio, then strained—put the dregs on the garden or back in the compost pile) will act as a slight anti-fungal remedy. Spraying with a mixture of 1 tablespoon baking soda plus a tablespoon of light horticultural oil (or dish soap) to 1 gallon of water will usually prevent new outbreaks of blackspot, rust, and powdery mildew. Safer™ sulfur-based fungicides work well on powdery mildew and rust, and can be used on a regular ten-day schedule to prevent new outbreaks of blackspot. As a last ditch effort, sulfur spray or powder smells a bit but is safe to use if applied on a regular basis when the temperatures are below $85°$. With any spray, be sure to cover both top and bottom of each leaf.

POWDERY MILDEW: Peak development is in cool, dry overcast conditions while the roses are in an active growth state. Overwinters in leaf buds. The young leaves appear blistered or curled, with a haze of powdery white fungus. Buds are also affected and may not open properly. Basic treatment is the same as with blackspot, except that this fungus doesn't thrive in contact with moisture and can also be controlled by water washes at weekly intervals.

Powdery mildew.

RUST: Peak development is during cool moist periods, especially during summer. Overwinters in leaf buds and within canes or on fallen leaves. Raised dots of orange or yellow can appear anywhere on the plant, but usually show first on the undersides of the leaves. Hot summers and cold winters keep this fungus pretty well controlled in most places. Basic treatment is the same as with blackspot.

Downy Mildew: Most commonly develops in cool conditions when the humidity is over eighty-five percent. This disease is less often seen than the first three but more disfiguring. Burgundy, copper, chocolate, and yellow splotches develop on the upper leaf surfaces, with a gray film of fungus on the underside. It's rather pretty at first, but does severe damage to the leaves and can also affect the calyxes of buds and kill small twigs. Good ventilation and removal of infected tissue are vital. Basic treatment is the same as with blackspot. Dormant oil sprays may be helpful in smothering overwintering spores if applied in winter, before the leaf buds begin to swell.

Canker: This is a less troublesome fungal disease, but unsightly. It usually enters where insects or natural abrasions or pruning stubs have left an opening, causing dark, swollen areas that can kill off a cane. The simplest treatment is mechanical pruning away and destruction of the diseased area. Rose varieties that are susceptible to canker can be protected by not leaving stubs during normal pruning and by ensuring that their canes are not chafing against each other or against other objects (such as a trellis or training tie).

Crown Gall: These hard, tumor-type growths are caused by bacteria in the soil, and are more likely to afflict grafted than own-root roses by entering at the bud union. They can also appear on various canes. The disease isn't a major garden pest, but no effective cure is available at the moment. Crown gall is debilitating rather than deadly, but it is contagious, so infected plants should be removed and destroyed along with the soil around the roots. If you are in a problem area for this disease, try to avoid injuring rose roots or crowns during planting or cultivating, and sterilize your pruning shears frequently by washing them with soap and water, then dipping the blades in alcohol and flaming them.

Rose Mosaic Virus: This is actually a group of viruses in roses, often represented by prunus necrotic ringspot virus, or PNRV. The foliage of an infected plant may have no symptoms at all (don't trust any rose grower that tells you they check their stock by just looking at it!), or it may display an interesting pattern of yellow lines in various "mosaic" patterns. Rose mosaic is debilitating, but not deadly—you don't need to discard a plant you like if it begins to manifest the symptomatic foliage patterns. Fortunately it's not easily contagious and can't be spread by the pruning shears or by sucking insects. This virus is continuously spread in the American rose trade by grafting bud wood of desirable varieties onto infected rootstock. This rootstock must have been propagated vegetatively from other infected plants—growing it from seed, as most foreign and some American nurseries do, produces disease-free plants. Unfortunately, if you have an own-root rose that was propagated from a plant infected by its rootstock, your plant probably also will be diseased. Checks for rose mosaic are performed by labs using the ELISA test. Bud wood can be cleaned up with heat treatment, also in the laboratory, to restore the breeding stock of an infected variety to health.

PNRV

Responsible rose growers are all involved in programs to get this disease under control. It creates poor quality roses, and there's no real excuse for its continued presence in American-grown roses. Growers listed in the reference section of this book are involved in active measures to prevent or clean up this disease in commercial rose stock.

Common rose pests and controls

Aphids: Eaten by lady beetles, lacewings, and many other predators. Repelled by garlic, dill, fennel, nasturtiums, catnip, coriander, tansy, marigolds. Hedgerows or walls help block them. A strong washing of the whole plant above and below the leaves with the hose will help to blast off much of the infestation; focus on succulent new growth as the majority will be found there. Ants often bite off their wings to keep them as honey cows, so aphids can't easily return to a rose when they get knocked off of it. Controlling ants helps control aphids (see "Fire Ants"). Safer™ insecticidal soap kills on contact but doesn't prevent reinfestation. A solution of two percent horticultural oil has more long-term effectiveness. High nitrogen levels in plants attract them, so use constant applications of a moderate nitrogen such as fish emulsion or seaweed to keep levels stable.

Cane Borers and Gall Wasps: Most insects (including rose-stem girdlers and rose-stem sawflies) whose larvae develop within rose canes are somewhat repelled by alliums. Individual swellings can be removed by pruning below the brown, infested area and destroying the larvae within the swollen tunnel or gall. There are also pheromone products available commercially that are effective against different types of borers. Gall wasps are most active during the summer and create swellings on the roots as well as the canes. These can also be pruned off mechanically.

Aphids attacking a bud.

Caterpillars and Sawfly Larvae: Parasitized by certain wasps—including yellow jackets, eaten by certain beetles and many birds. Repelled by some petunias (try the old-fashioned reseeding kind). Sawfly larvae often roll a leaf around themselves. It's mildly enter-taining to hand-pick these voracious leafeaters and step on them or drop them into a bucket of soapy water—though you can just spray each one with insecticidal soap. They're susceptible to *Bacillus thuringensis* var. *kurstaki* (BTK) when applied as directed on the container. Not all caterpillars are bad—obviously you want to preserve varieties that turn into interesting but-terflies. My rule of thumb is that caterpillars on perennials or annuals get looked up and identified, but if they're eating leaves or flowers on my rose bushes it's okay to feed them to the chickens.

CATS: Less damaging than dogs. For some reason a sleeping cat doesn't seem to compact the soil much, and they spread their donations around so widely that plants rarely get burned. A trap crop such as catnip will help keep them out of newly planted areas, as will a coarse mulch that *doesn't* remind them of kitty litter.

DEER: In lieu of a six- to eight-foot fence or electrified wire, try dou-ble-fencing the garden (with host plants for beneficial insects in the extra space) or letting a tangle of large roses naturalize around the borders. Deer like to see where they're jumping and have a clear shot at it. Commercial deer repellents such as Hinder™ work reasonably well when left in small pots (such as tuna fish cans) around the garden. The pots need to be partly covered so that the odor escapes but the rain can't dilute it too much. Bars of deodorant soap have also been suggested as effective, but they do look strange hanging in the rose bushes and they do have a strong smell at odds with that of the garden. In my personal experience, human urine, applied around the perimeter (full strength) and around chosen roses (well-diluted) every few weeks or after a rain, does better than anything except a dog in the yard. The ingredients—though not certified for use on food crops—are unquestionably organic, the odor is undetectable to us, the deer don't like it and the roses do.

DOGS—OTHER PEOPLE'S: Get a fence. Or set upside-down mouse-traps around an area that needs extra protection: the surprise may shock them into digging elsewhere. Your *own* dogs, being more intelligent and bet-ter behaved, will be perfectly able to learn the command "Out of the bed!" if it is offered consistently and they have some clue—such as the presence of edging or flashing—to help them determine what *is* the bed and what *isn't*. Peeing on plants isn't altogether bad (lots of nitrogen) as long as you notice and can dilute it fairly soon to prevent burning.

FIRE ANTS: Confine control to areas where they are a serious prob-lem, as they are an important part of the overall insect balance. Fire ants help control ticks, ground wasps, boll weevils, and other pests. In the garden they damage not only the gardener but the plants in whose roots they make their nests. Most good nurseries and feed stores carry the hormone Logic™, a very effective control to limit fire ant breeding that is under study for fur-ther organic certification. This bait can't be used within a limited radius of food crops at the moment if you're a commercial organic gardener, but unless you have direct runoff into a body of water it's excellent for private gardens. Logic™ works best when applied as directed on the label, in late April after the ants have come down from their mating flights and again in August. For rapid temporary action, there are several new products with d-limonene and linalool that work well. Fire ants can be persuaded to at least move out of a garden bed by being regularly disturbed with a strong stream of water from the hose.

Fleas: These irritating creatures affect the garden environment by driving homeowners crazy, causing them to break organic training and hire someone to spray yard and house with chemical controls. Treating the indoors with the hormone Precor™ (also available as Vigren™) is *very* effective: it prevents new fleas developing for about seven months and alleviates most of the human misery. To rid the house of any stray adult fleas, regular vacuuming works beautifully, with the vacuum emptied after each use. Bathing and flea combing will keep infestations down on pets. For the outdoors, beneficial nematodes that specifically parasitize fleas are now available at many nurseries and feed stores and through mail-order catalogs. These do an excellent job in the yard if applied during the wet spring or fall season. They die if they dry out, so they must be reapplied after a drought. Diatomaceous earth, insecticidal soaps, and pet sprays using the citrus-peel extracts d-limonene and linalool are helpful for particularly bad infestations that spread to paved outdoor areas and doormats. Reapply after each rainstorm.

Grasshoppers: Eaten by tiger beetles, yellow jacket wasps. Repelled by barrier plantings. Confused by trap crops. They can be very effectively controlled (as can crickets) by applications of the protozoa *Nosema locustae*, sold as NOLO™ bait or Semaspore™. This useful disease should be applied when the grasshoppers are one third grown to be most effective. It's expensive, but doesn't have to be applied very often after the first two years because it stays in the population: grasshoppers are cannibalistic and pass it along by eating each other.

Foraging beetle. (*Liz Druitt*)

Japanese Beetles, Rose Chafers, Cucumber Beetles: Eaten (the ground-dwelling larvae) by beneficial nematodes. Repelled by catnip, garlic, and geraniums. Borage acts as a trap crop. Hand-picking keeps the numbers of all beetles down to bearable levels. Wandering through the garden in early morning and tapping cold beetles into a bucket of soapy water can be strangely rewarding to the primal self—not unlike shooting ducks at dawn. Milky spore (*Bacillus popilliae*) disease is very effective for Japanese beetles if you have a real problem. Commercial beetle traps seem to attract more beetles to the area and aren't worth the effort, though barrier plantings will probably deter some. Bioneem™, the systemic insecticide made from neem tree oil, is recommended in catalogs and rose group newsletters but is not approved for organic application, and it would be a last resort because it's still uncertain how much damage it might do to larval populations of lady beetles and other beneficial insects. (My favorite control method is the "Spikes O' Death" lawn aerator sandals. You have to water the lawn first, then tromp across it several times to pierce a significant number of beetle larvae. Good for the soil in general and fun to explain to the neighbors.) Most beetles respond to the same basic controls. There's no value in trying to destroy your entire beetle population, no matter how much you hate to find them in your roses, as this will also destroy a natural balance. The adults make good bird food and the grubs support several native and introduced predators.

LEAFHOPPERS: Eaten by damsel bugs, assassin bugs. May be repelled by alliums, tansy, wormwood. These fast-moving, little sucking insects usually cause little damage to a healthy rose bush, but a heavy population of them can affect the foliage. They're susceptible to insecticidal soaps or a two percent horticultural oil solution if you can manage to spray before they either jump off or whip around to the other side of the stem.

MOLES, MICE, ETC.: Deep flashing—eighteen to twenty four inches below ground and four to six inches above ground—will keep out most burrowing rodents. Wormwood is somewhat repellent. *Lycoris radiata*, the red spider lily that blooms in fall, is also a repellent if the bulbs are planted as a barrier around the garden. Rodents don't eat narcissus bulbs, either— they're toxic—so you can make a nice multi-seasonal edging by mixing them with the lycoris. Moles are serious predators of pest insects and help aerate the soil, so the goal should be just to keep them out of garden beds rather than destroying them entirely. They like earthworms but do little damage to plants, except that their tunneling can sometimes leave roots hanging in the air to dry out, and more omnivorous mice may borrow the tunnels for their own feasting. Most areas—lawns, for example—recover easily from mole damage, and moles are such voracious feeders that they can only afford to stick around if you have a serious pest insect problem to support them. Balance your bugs and you'll have less trouble with tunnels.

PILLBUGS, SOWBUGS: They don't like dry conditions, so water early in day when the sun can evaporate any excess moisture. If you have a real problem with them, switch from fine to coarse mulch to avoid making a dense, damp layer where they can hide. Disturb soil around seedlings during day to catch them—they're easy for kids to pick up and drown in soapy water. A two-inch-wide sprinkling of diatomaceous earth around new seedlings will help, if it doesn't get wet. These interesting crustaceans are good at processing decayed organic material and they don't do much damage to mature plants, but they can be very hard on weak or succulent seedlings and fruits or vegetables that rest on damp ground. If you want to know exactly what you have, pillbugs curl up when disturbed, sowbugs can't.

ROOT KNOT NEMATODES: Alliums help repel them. Non-beneficial nematodes are only a problem in specific areas. Your extension agent will have information on local control methods. In locations with severe infestations you can help protect your rose roots from these microscopic, knot-forming invaders by growing them in containers (with drainage holes) sunk into the garden beds. Many species of nematodes are highly beneficial in combating other pests. Commercial products containing bacteria that combat plant-parasitic nematodes may soon be available.

ROSE MIDGES: Parasitized by some beneficial nematodes. Repelled by alliums and strong-scented herbs. It's the minuscule white maggots of the midge that do the damage in warm weather, causing growing tips and buds to crisp and shrivel as if blackened by a fire. Prune off infected material as soon as early as possible and destroy it to prevent further generations.

SCALES: Eaten by lacewings, mealybug destroyers. Related to aphids, mealybugs, and whiteflies, these sucking insects look more like a bed of flat round oysters. They may be repelled by the same companion plants as aphids when immature and still mobile. Rub off mature, visible scales with gloves or a toothbrush or a cotton swab (this can be dipped in alcohol). Spray tops and bottoms of leaves on an infected plant with insecticidal soap to kill unprotected larval stages.

SNAILS AND SLUGS: Eaten by predator snail. Repelled by wormwood, maybe by fennel mulch. They enjoy living under ivy and succulent groundcovers. Use traps to collect them: small boards will collect them underneath, as will inverted (hollow) grapefruit halves set out in garden overnight or slices of raw potato. Drop the night's catch into soapy water, then add the corpses to the compost pile. They really will crawl into "beer pits," but a shallow dish of mixed yeast and water will work just as well. Copper is toxic to them, so if you live in a horribly infested area, consider a copper strip (commercially available through some nurseries and catalogs) as part of your garden edging.

SPIDER MITES, PEST MITES: Parasitized by predatory mites. Repelled by dill. Dislike sulfur. They can be kept well controlled by a hard water wash from the garden hose above and especially below the leaves; they dislike humidity and tend to attack during hot, dry weather. They're also susceptible to direct applications of Safer™ insecticidal soap or a two percent solution of horticultural oil spray. Pest mite damage shows up as a dusting of pale dots on the leaf surface. Fine webbing can be seen on the undersurface of the leaf, and the microscopic mites—which come in a variety of colors, depending upon species—can be seen with a magnifying lens. Tapping an infested leaf over a sheet of white paper will often produce a scattering of what looks like mobile ground pepper.

SPITTLE BUGS: Eaten by yellow jackets. Easy to spot by the foamy "spit" nests they make on plant stems. They rarely do severe damage, but if their appearance is objectionable they can be removed with a clear conscience. They knock off easily with a hard spray from the hose. Squashing them in their wet foam hideouts (use gloves if you prefer) is a more permanent solution. You can spray with insecticidal soap or a two percent horticultural oil solution, but it has to penetrate the spit to be useful.

'Mermaid' with thrips and cucumber beetle.

THRIPS: Eaten by lacewings, damsel bugs, pirate bugs, and predatory mites. Beneficial nematodes are effective because thrips pupate in the soil. Repelled by alliums. They don't like wet conditions and can be drowned easily, so a good water wash with the hose will keep populations down. Keeping the soil moisture constant with good irrigation can also help prevent them. Insecticidal soap only works for a while; they become resistant. When offered a diversity of plants in the garden, and particularly outside it, thrips will often prefer weedy plants and keep problem infestations to a minimum. Thrips are particularly attracted to the pale flowers where their damage is most visible, like cats that choose to shed on clothing of a color that contrasts well with their fur. If you're using roses in arrangements or for cooking and think they might have thrips, let them sit (with the stems wrapped in something moist) on white paper towels for a little while first. The majority of the insects will migrate to the paler surface and save you all kinds of embarrassment.

WHITEFLY: Eaten by *Encarsia formosa* mini-wasps. Repelled by nasturtiums. Attracted to the yellow of Rustoleum #659; make a trap for enclosed sites by spraying a board with that paint, then lightly coating it with a mixture of two parts Vaseline to one part dish or insecticidal soap and placing it near the plants. Wash off the trap and recoat it as it gets covered with the insects. You can also vacuum off the underside of leaves with a hand vacuum in early mornings while they're gathered, then freeze the vacuum bag (or the whole machine) for two days to kill them. If populations of these sucking insects seem to be rising, try spraying the roses with a two percent horticultural oil solution—always after a good watering, so the plants are not moisture stressed. The horticultural oil will smother many insects and make it harder for them to get established on the foliage. A balance of beneficial insects and good diversity in the garden often keep this pest from getting to problem levels.

YELLOW JACKETS: Hose 'em away from the nest at a safe distance with a stream of water, pick off the nest while they're gone and dispose of it. Move slowly and be respectful: their sting may be fierce, but they do have a function as beneficial predators, especially of caterpillars. Perhaps because they are also seasonally fond of sweet nectar (and soft drinks or cake, as picnickers can attest) these wasps find the interiors of large bush or climbing roses particularly attractive as nesting sites. If you know they are around, check carefully before pruning.

ROSE CLASSES

AND QUICK REFERENCE CHART

hoosing roses for your garden can be a lot more interesting than merely going to the local nursery and looking over the Hybrid Teas and Floribundas. There are fifty-six official classes of roses listed by the American Rose Society, with varying numbers of cultivars in each class. Each class has characteristic botanical and behavioral traits, based on the genetic background of its cultivars. As a result, there's an overwhelming selection of rose varieties in existence with an incredibly wide range of garden talents. Fortunately for poor confused gardeners, not all of them are currently available in commerce, and not all of them will perform well in every type of climate and soil. To ease the task of selection a little, here's a brief explanation of some of the terms you may hear while rose shopping, plus a description of the basic traits of some classes that have cultivars particularly well suited to warm-climate gardening.

The accompanying chart arranges the 175 roses described in the next chapter (just the tip of a very large iceberg in terms of those that can be grown organically) into groups by garden size, with general suggestions of the most appropriate growing zones. Remember that every rose will be affected by the place it's planted—varieties that stay at five feet in Dallas may grow to ten feet in New Orleans or Tallahassee—so adjust for your own locale.

HYBRID: Hybrid is not a bad word. It just means that a rose is bred from two parents. Species roses, found wild in nature, are self-fertile and reproduce themselves from seed. The vast majority of garden roses in existence—those that aren't actual species themselves—have always been a result of original crosses between various species roses that were then

An arbor of 'Buff Beauty'.

crossed with each other, ad infinitum. Health, fragrance, form, and foliage are all affected by the genetic make-up of the individual hybrid, and the final selection of commercial plants is affected by the interests of the breeder. If, like Ralph Moore, Harvey Davidson, Dr. Robert Basye, David Austin, or Alan Meilland, to name a very few of the many good modern breeders, you're interested in more than just the shape and color of the flower, your hybrids will be excellent garden plants. Even in the single, much maligned class of Hybrid Teas there are far more good garden roses than bad ones, and the ratio will keep improving as concerned gardeners continue to let the hybridizers know what they want in a rose.

'Rosamundi'

SPORT: A sport, horticulturally, is a genetic mutation, not a game. Roses are a bit unstable as a rule, and many varieties have been known to throw out an unusual cane or two bearing double flowers instead of single, single instead of double, odd-colored blossoms, and even climbing or dwarf forms of the original cultivar. In the South, where we have a history of appreciating the eccentricities of our loved ones, this tendency could certainly never be considered a fault. In fact, many sports are propagated—you can do that by taking your cuttings from the new cane—and introduced into commerce themselves. 'Souvenir de St. Anne's', as an example, is the beautiful and nearly single sport of the very double 'Souvenir de la Malmaison', and the striped 'Rosamundi' is the sport of the solid-colored 'Apothecary's Rose'.

DISEASE RESISTANCE: Most roses are disease resistant—somewhere. And most are disease prone somewhere else. Blackspot is not just one fungus, but many variations on a fungal theme. Wherever you garden, you'll have your own kind of blackspot, plus your own micro-environment of soil and climate and whatever local pests and diseases come with that environment. As a result, you should take all "disease-resistant" labeling with a grain of salt until you've grown a variety for yourself. You should also never be afraid to try a rose you yearn for: it may do just fine in your yard even though your neighbor can't grow it. The only rose I've never seen with blackspot anywhere is the Chestnut Rose, *Rosa roxburghii.*

FOUND ROSE: A found rose is exactly what it implies: a rose someone found. In general, these are roses that have been out of commerce a while, so their correct cultivar names are not easy to trace. If a found rose is reintroduced into commerce, it's given a study name, marked by double quotes instead of the single quotes of a registered name. An example is the found Bourbon rose, "Maggie." With continuous dialogue and research carried on by assorted rosarians some found roses are eventually identified; then their study names are replaced with the correct names. Found roses are extremely valuable because they are almost without exception tough varieties that have survived for long periods of time. You may or may not want to grow some of these roses yourself, but it's important to keep them available for study and for future breeding. If you're interested in these foundlings and other aspects of rose preservation, you may want to join the Heritage Rose Foundation (see Resources).

ANTIQUE ROSE: Antique is a non-specific term in roses, simply designating any roses that have been around for a while and have nostalgic associations. The important term in rose classification is "Old Garden Rose," signifying a rose cultivar belonging to a class established before 1867, the introduction date of the first Hybrid Tea. If you want to know whether your roses are antiques, you can use the classic car timeline and assume anything over twenty-five years of age fits. My personal rule of thumb is that the rose has to be older than I am before it can be considered antique.

ENGLISH ROSE: This is another non-specific term because it has no official standing at this time. It's used in marketing to designate any of the modern roses introduced by British breeder David Austin. These lovely roses do possess certain botanical similarities because they've been selected for certain kinds of flowers and fragrances, but they still retain so many differences that rosarians are uncomfortable in grouping them as a specific class, nor do they feel right about ignoring the many fine varieties produced by other notable English hybridizers. Austin's cultivars are currently included in the broadly defined Shrub class of roses.

GROUNDCOVER ROSE: Some roses have a very relaxed habit of growth that allows them to spread out wider than they are tall. These grow beautifully weeping in containers, trailing over retaining walls, and spilling from hanging baskets. Groundcover is not a class designation, but a garden form like "arching shrub" or "climber." Roses that grow well when encouraged to hang down or spread vertically come from a number of different classes, as the following chart will demonstrate. The only puzzle is why these generally prickly plants are marketed as "low-maintenance lawn replacements." They are not what I would choose either to walk on or to weed, they rarely offer evergreen coverage, and they usually need some grooming to stay at their best, just like any rose.

PILLAR ROSE: As with groundcover roses, this term describes a form, not a class. Any rose with reasonably flexible canes long enough to wrap around a support—it doesn't have to be an actual pillar—can be used as a pillar rose. The name implies only that the rose canes are moderate in length (say 5 to 10 feet rather than 15 to 20 feet) and won't quickly overshoot their designated support.

BUDDING AND GRAFTING: Budding, or "bud-grafting," is the process of slicing axillary buds from a scion, or shoot, of a desired rose, and sliding it into a T-shaped slit in the bark of a more vigorous understock variety. The bud is fastened into place with a specialized band, and the following spring the understock is cut back to just above the bud union so that the desired rose can grow straight and develop into a full bush. This is the most economical way to make a lot of new roses from a small amount of material, though the whole process takes over a year to produce a saleable rose. Grafting, or binding the entire scion to the rootstock at a precisely cut angle, is faster but is also more difficult and this process uses more material for the same result. When you see either term in a rose catalog, such as in a description of "grafted standards" (which are those interesting-looking "tree" roses), bud-grafting is probably what is meant.

*R*OSE CLASSES

"Nowhere is this lovely flower seen in such perfection, and in such abundance, as in our own sunny South...[but] variety is wanting. Few are grown save the Perpetuals, and some others of the more common sorts. Perhaps a short sketch of the different families into which the Rose is divided, directing attention to the peculiar beauties of each, may help to remedy this defect."

These words of Mississippi nurseryman Thomas Affleck, written in his 1851/52 catalog, remain interestingly accurate today. Because there is such

'Mrs. B.R. Cant'

comes along. They are also distinguished by several members, such as 'Archduke Charles' and 'Mutabilis', whose flowers start out in pale colors and darken to crimson. Plant forms range from dwarf bushes to moderate and large ones, to vigorous climbers. They are tolerant of alkalinity, clay soils, unending heat, and humidity—in fact, they thrive in zones 6 or 7 through 10 and could have been created specifically for Southern gardens. They do so well, in fact, that there is a certain confusion of identity among the myriad red Chinas collected in gardens, cemeteries, and old plantings from Bermuda all the way across to California.

TEAS: Very similar in history and cultivation requirements to the China roses, members of this class tend to form chunky, v-shaped shrubs well-covered with foliage and flowers, though there are also some excellent climbers. The flowers are generally pastels, with a few good reds, and uniquely scented with an earthy, slightly acrid perfume that reminds some people of tea. Like the Chinas, several varieties are known for starting out pale—yellow, in particular—and darkening in the sun, usually to pink. Teas are the backbone of the warm climate garden, and there are many of them that have been collected from old plantings and are so wonderful they've been put back in commerce with just their temporary study names. Perhaps because they are so unswerving in their general commitment to always doing good, there are two areas in which they tend to act like Christian martyrs: if pruned too hard (more than half the bush cut away at once) they may sulk for a season with few flowers, and they almost always grow slowly at the

'Lamarque', a Noisette.

first, blooming heavily but keeping small until they've been in your garden for two or three years. Teas are generally hardy in zones 6 or 7 through 10.

NOISETTES: Hybrids of Chinas, the *Rosa moschata*, and Teas, these tender roses are the third class which no Southern gardener should be without. They were first bred in Charleston, South Carolina, then developed fur-

"Maggie," a found Bourbon.

ther in France, but they belong in a warm climate as they do best between zones 7 and 10. Some early Noisettes are erect shrubs, but the majority are large climbers, known for their drooping clusters of perfumed pastel flowers. They are tolerant of clay soils and easy to incorporate into any garden plan; just keep the supports strong and the roll of jute handy to keep up with them as they increase in glory.

BOURBONS: Named for the French ruling class, not the mint julep ingredient, these roses are further hybrids of Chinese and European varieties. They tend to have large flowers, richly scented of "rose" perfume, on leggy bushes, though some are chunky shrubs. They grow excellently as far as zone 9, then they struggle a bit more with blackspot and balling. The varieties described in the following chapter are among the most reliable repeat-bloomers and the most heat-resistant of the class. The found Bourbon "Maggie," is probably one of the most widely known of all old Southern roses, having been collected from Virginia to Florida across to California.

HYBRID PERPETUALS: These are the pre-twentieth-century equivalent of Hybrid Teas, in that they tend towards huge flowers, stiffly awkward bushes, and blackspot. The differences are the general presence of deliciously strong fragrance combined with less reliable repeat-blooming. HP's do better in the cool zones, but a number of them thrive for us at least into zone 9, and they're fun to grow—worth a little extra fuss and bother. They also win a lot at rose shows. Treat them like European roses, with a little afternoon shade and a cool root zone, to get the best performance.

*M*ODERN GARDEN ROSE CLASSES

There are a lot more modern rose classes than simply Hybrid Teas and Floribundas, and they include some of the best garden roses ever developed.

A stunning collection of Rugosas: 'Hansa', 'Blanc Double de Coubert', *Rosa rugosa alba*—and the Large-Flowered Climber 'Madame Grégoire Staechelin'. In Jane White's garden in Lynchburg, Virginia.

bloom best in massive spring and fall flushes, followed by good production of hips.

HYBRID RUGOSAS: These are just what they should be: crosses with the cold-hardy, spicy-scented Japanese sea-coast roses. Foliage tends to be rough and deeply veined, and the flowers tend to be shades of pink, crimson, mauve, and white, with petals that look like crumpled silk. Hybrid rugosas are very tough roses in the North, but not all of them thrive in the dense soils of the South. 'Mary Manners' and 'Sarah Van Fleet' are two outstanding exceptions, and many of the others do beautifully at least into zone 9 if you give them light soils with good drainage. The species cultivar *R. rugosa rubra* is one of the best all-time hip producers, and many of the varieties, like 'Hansa', are not far behind.

LARGE-FLOWERED CLIMBERS AND RAMBLERS: Even though these are two different classes because of the genetic heritage of the cultivars included, basically these are all climbing roses. LCL's are likely to have larger flowers and stiffer canes, while Ramblers tend toward clusters and flexibility, but there are as many crossovers as between Pop and Country Music. Both classes do well in the South to zone 9 and beyond—often better than related shrub roses—and they tolerate a wide range of growing conditions. Select among them for climbers of the right size and the right amount of

flexibility for the space and type of training you plan to do: there are so many possibilities you can almost certainly find the sort of plant you need with the kind of flower you like attached to it.

MINIATURES: Miniature roses are almost the only modern roses almost always sold on their own roots, so they're great

'Blaze', a favorite Large-flowered Climber.

for use in the garden and rarely (except for some of the grafted standards) affected by rose mosaic virus. Many are healthy, energetically flowering plants, and a percentage can be carefully selected for fragrance as well. They tend to be small plants, designed to be under 2 feet, which means just under 3 feet in zone 9 and who knows in zone 10? They are still fairly small bushes and can be used as accents, low borders or *en masse* for effect. There are climbing and trailing varieties available that do well in hanging baskets or as softly sprawling underplantings for larger roses. They can be kept in quite small containers for ever if taken out and root-pruned every few years as you would a Bonsai tree. Minis are available in a remarkable assortment of colors, and they're so easy to breed and grow that the cultivars are multiplying rapidly. Keep them groomed and free-

These Miniatures—'Millie Walters' and 'Phyllis Shackleford'—show their landscape versatility.

flowering by pinching or clipping away spent blooms, as you would with a begonia. Not all Minis are fond of constant heat and heavy soil, but they are fairly reliable to zone 9 and with a little (excuse the pun) experimentation you should be able to find a number of good ones for your specific environment. The only problem for which they need to be monitored is spider mites; their tiny, low-to-the-ground foliage is hard to

The Shrub rose, 'Belinda's Dream'.

reach with a hard water spray, so you have to pay careful attention if a mite infestation starts to develop.

SHRUBS AND KORDESII: The Shrub class is an amazing mixture of forms, from small bush to rabid climber, as if all the good garden roses no one knew how to classify ended up in this category. As a result, it can be one of the most fun for browsing—it contains some real treasures, including most of David Austin's roses. Kordesii roses are a separate class because they're hybrids or descendants of *R. kordesii*, but their garden forms include

Small Roses (Continued)

NAME	CLASS	COLOR	FRAGRANCE	SIZE (FEET)	REPEAT BLOOM	HIPS	SHADE TOLERANCE	BEST IN ZONES
Rise 'n' Shine	Miniature	yellow	*	1–3	yes	no	some	5–9
Showbiz	Floribunda	bright scarlet	no	2–3	yes	no	some	6–9
Starina	Miniature	orange-scarlet	*	1–3	yes	no	some	6–9
Sweet Chariot	Miniature	mauve pink	**	1–3	yes	no	some	6–9
Winsome	Miniature	mauve	**	1–3	yes	no	some	6–9

Mid-Size Roses (3 to 4 Feet)

NAME	CLASS	COLOR	FRAGRANCE	SIZE (FEET)	REPEAT BLOOM	HIPS	SHADE TOLERANCE	BEST IN ZONES
Alain Blanchard	Gallica	crimson streaked with mauve	**	3–4	no	some	some	4–8
Alec's Red	Hybrid Tea	medium red	***	3–4	yes	some	some	6–9
Angel Face	Floribunda	mauve-lavender	***	2–4	yes	yes	some	6–9
Caldwell Pink	found Polyantha	blue pink	no	3–4	yes	no	no	6–9
Clotilde Soupert	Polyantha	rose pink to white	***	3–4	yes	no	good	6–9
Comtesse du Cayla	China	crimson with orange wash	***	2–4	yes	some	some	7–10
Crested Moss	Moss	medium pink	***	3–4	no	some	some	4–8
Dainty Bess	Hybrid Tea	silvery pink	**	3–4	yes	some	some	6–9
Dame de Coeur	Hybrid Tea	red	***	3–4	yes	some	some	6–9

Mid-Size Roses (Continued)

Name	Class	Color	Fragrance	Size (Feet)	Repeat Bloom	Hips	Shade Tolerance	Best in Zones
Double Delight	Hybrid Tea	red and white	***	3–4	yes	some	some	6–9
Ducher	China	white	**	3–4	yes	some	some	7–10
Fair Bianca	Shrub	white	***	3–4	yes	some	some	6–9
The Fairy	Polyantha	light pink	*	3×4	yes	no	some	5–9
Frau Dagmar Hartopp	Hybrid Rugosa	pale pink	***	3–4	yes	yes	some	4–9
Gabrielle Privat	Polyantha	dark pink	no	3–4	yes	no	some	5–9
Green Rose	China	green	*	3–4	yes	no	some	6–10
Gruss an Aachen	Floribunda	cream and apricot	*	3–4	yes	no	some	5–9
Hermosa	China	blue pink	***	3–4	yes	some	some	6–10
Iceberg	Floribunda	white	*	3–5	yes	some	some	6–9
Impatient	Floribunda	orange	*	3–4	yes	no	some	6–9
La Belle Sultane	Gallica	dark crimson mauve	***	3–5	no	yes	some	4–9
Le Vésuve	China	shades of dark and light pink	**	3–4	yes	some	some	7–10
Madame Louis Lévêque	Moss	bright salmon pink	***	3–4	some repeat	no	some	5–8
Margaret Merril	Floribunda	blush white	***	3–4	yes	no	some	6–9
Marie Pavié	Polyantha	blush white	***	3–4	yes	no	yes	5–9
Mrs. Oakley Fisher	Hybrid Tea	copper yellow	***	3–4	yes	some	some	6–9
Oklahoma	Hybrid Tea	very dark red	***	3–4	yes	yes	some	6–9

ROSES THAT THRIVE IN ORGANIC GARDENS

ABRAHAM DARBY
Shrub. Introduced 1990.

The actual registration of this rose is under breeder David Austin's original code name of AUScot, and that's how to find it in conscientious reference books. It's one of the most rewarding of his rose introductions, though it may seem too recent to have proved itself. It was introduced in Europe in 1985, so it's already been grown there for a decade.

'Abraham Darby' was named for a founder of the Industrial Revolution, but a softer, sweeter, more luxurious rose would be hard to find. Peach pink on the outer petals with a coppery center, the cupped and multipetaled flowers have a perfume so sinfully rich it almost seems fattening. 'Abraham Darby' produces relaxed, flexible canes in the 5- to 7-foot range, making it an awkward bush no matter how firmly you prune it back. It performs excellently as a pillar or pegged rose, however, and can be used as a moderate climber. The foliage is medium green and covers the plant well, providing an appropriately lush backdrop for the huge flowers. 'Abraham Darby's' blooms stand heat and sun very well, and I've seen it thrive in alkaline clay soils that drove more disciplined plants to chlorosis.

ALAIN BLANCHARD
Gallica. Introduced 1839.

'Alain Blanchard' is one of the Gallicas that can handle the warmer temperatures of the South, though you might expect a rose this highly colored to be highly strung as well. The semi-double flowers look as if they were each handspun on a potter's wheel while the crafter spattered their crimson petals with mauve and purple dye. The stamens make a solid golden center that gives the eye some sane relief from the "mad" coloring of the petals. This rose makes a bush about 3½ feet high and arching, comprised of slender canes that curve over with the weight of spring flowers and foliage. It works well tucked into a middle position in the bed, near enough to the front so that the flowers can trail over artistically into the pathway and away from direct prominence when the foliage looks its worst at the end of the summer. Even though 'Alain Blanchard' only blooms in the spring, it's a healthy, fragrant and unique plant to round out a collection of roses and offers hips and colorful foliage for the autumn season. It can be underplanted with such companions as bright spring bulbs and heat-loving blue *Salvia farinacea* to fill in any gaps in performance and accent the beauties of the rose itself.

ALEC'S RED
Hybrid Tea. Introduced 1973.

Sensible breeding can't help but be appreciated. This gorgeous, sturdy, and fragrant rose inherited all the best qualities of its bloodlines: flower form and perfume from 'Fragrant Cloud', color and health from 'Dame de Coeur'. Actually, both the large, very double flower and the strong red color are better than in either parent, but it can only be a positive sign when the child excels in this way. 'Alec's Red' is only recently available in the United States, but it has won a number of awards in Europe while we've been waiting for it. The large and very double flowers are competition quality, but the bush needs only ordinary care to thrive in the organic garden. It is a little stockier and wider growing than many Hybrid Teas, which results in more canes with more flowers to enjoy. Average height is only about 4 feet, so it can be used in a number of design areas, including containers. 'Alec's Red' and the pink 'Belinda's Dream' are two roses that might have been made specifically to comfort gardeners who can't decide between the healthy vigor of older garden shrub roses and the massive, high-centered flowers of the Hybrid Teas.

ALFRED COLOMB
Hybrid Perpetual. Introduced 1865.

It's a constant joke among rosarians that this class of roses is far more hybrid than perpetual, but 'Alfred Colomb' does its best to regain some honor for the family. Leggy, awkwardly branched, and inclined to flop its flowers on the mulch rather than hold them erect, it is still a beautiful and valuable plant. It can be easily bound around a pillar with gorgeous results, for the foliage and flowers only become more numerous when the 5- to 6-foot canes are wrapped or otherwise bent from the vertical position. Even in the garden those that have relaxed along the surface of the bed are loaded with blooms while the ones up waving in air are much more sparsely covered—a natural lesson in how to get the best from your roses.

The flowers would be worth waiting for even if 'Alfred Colomb' didn't turn them out in regular cycles throughout the growing season. The large, tightly packed, almost quartered blooms are dusty strawberry on the inside, dark crimson on the backs of the petals, and the fragrance is intensely damask. 'Alfred Colomb' has proved its vigor by growing and blooming well under the combined onslaught of heat, sun, and grasshoppers.

petals dry less attractively because the white turns brown.

As a garden plant the 'Apothecary's Rose' remains reliable, at least in zones 7 and 8. When overcome by moist heat it will shed leaves freely, though they come back well in the fall. It suckers and sends up individual new canes about 4 feet tall, so there's the possibility of a small thicket forming around the original bush in ideal conditions. It will do best with good soil and drainage, and with afternoon shade and full morning sun. Actually, even if you decide to plant it in a full sun herb garden on the south coast you can get reasonable results if you mulch well and keep a soaker hose on it all summer so the roots stay cool.

ARCHDUKE CHARLES
China. Introduced before 1837.

This is not just a good garden shrub, it's sort of a floral Rorsach test. Since the middle of the last century rosarians have been describing 'Archduke Charles', but at least half of them do it backwards. When the flowers are new, the soft crimson guard petals open to display all the pale pink insides. Then the whole blossom gradually darkens in the sun, until it's soft crimson all over. I've watched this closely, because so many descriptions involve the flower starting out red and fading to pale pink. I know which way I believe it happens, but it's up to you to observe your own bush. Whichever way you decide, I can't tell you what it means, but I can tell you, you won't be alone.

'Archduke Charles' reaches about 4 feet in height and is slightly narrower than it is tall. The double flowers are produced constantly, in the best China tradition, though summer specimens are not very exciting. Spring and fall blossoms are truly beautiful in their subtle changes, with a pleasantly sweet fragrance. They last well in flower arrangements, having slightly more substantial petals than some of the other Chinas. A longtime favorite, 'Archduke Charles' is a common rose to find in old cemeteries.

AUTUMN DAMASK
Damask. Introduced before 1819.

When rose authorities suggest that 'Autumn Damask' was in gardens before 1819, they mean about *two thousand years* before. Even though the nineteenth-century date was chosen as the first reliable description of the rose in commerce, it seems to be a good candidate for the Roman "Four-Seasons Rose of Paestum." Most of the few roses available to Europeans before 1790 came out of dormancy to bloom for one season and go dormant again, trying to make it through long cold winters. A cultivar that rebloomed as this does, especially with these double pink flowers of exquisite perfume, would obviously have been prized and preserved by enthusiastic gardeners. Besides, it is still known as "Rose des Quatre Saisons" in modern French, echoing the ancient Latin name. There is a wonderful white mossy sport, 'Perpetual White Moss', whose "Quatre Saisons Blanc Mousseux" pseudonym supports the theory.

Another common name for 'Autumn Damask' is "Rose of Castille," and under this alias it has naturalized in New Mexico, where it and the "Yellow Rose of Texas," ('Harison's Yellow') grow like weeds in driveways and drainage ditches. It will bloom a little better in the garden if the 4- to 6-foot-long prickly canes are pruned into bushiness, pegged, or trained on a fence. Hot sun doesn't bother it, but the humidity that promotes fungal diseases can be a problem. As with many other old European rose varieties, 'Autumn Damask' will grow very successfully if it is mulched and given extra water during the worst of the summer through a nice cool soaker hose or drip irrigation at the roots.

BABY FAURAX
Polyantha. Introduced 1924.

The correct pronunciation for this little rose is "four ax," but I've rarely heard anyone say it that way; usually it comes out "four oh," and everyone knows what you mean. The rose itself is so small that it would be introduced today as a Miniature. It rarely passes 2½ feet in height, with a full, bushy little compact form. The tiny purplish flowers are quite double, but they open flat to show gold stamens set in a small white eye, and there's an occasional white streak in the petals. They're produced in clusters all over the bush, and they're even fragrant, though you have to catch them just opening to be sure.

'Baby Faurax' is a tough and reliable rose that can be used anywhere in the garden. The mauve flowers look good with the silvers and grey greens of the herb patch, or clustered to hide the naked ankles of a taller pale pink rose. It can be left in a pot forever or used to brightly edge the floral state map you've planted in the curve of the driveway. This rose is not at all fussy: rough dead-heading with light shears will keep it always in bloom, or you can groom it carefully into a handsome, if diminutive, display plant. It will root easily from cuttings, so you only need one to get started on a whole bed full.

BALLERINA
Hybrid Musk. Introduced 1937.

A hard worker in the landscape, this is a rose whose toughness is belied by its delicate appearance. 'Ballerina' is often pruned into a round little bush covered with large pink clusters or trained on a low trellis, but if there's room in the garden it's much better left to grow to its natural form here in the South. It will become a 4- or 5-foot-high and equally wide arching shrub, well covered with foliage except at the very bottom. When the canes are left long, the weight of the flower clusters can be overbalanced by

passing breezes so that the rose lives up to its dancing name. The musk-scented individual flowers are quite small, single, with a white eye centered on the clean pink petals. They form substantial clusters at or near the ends of the canes, and are replaced at petal fall by clusters of tiny orange hips.

As with other Hybrid Musk roses, 'Ballerina' is tough, disease resistant, and tolerant of both full sun and partial shade. As long as it gets at least three or four hours of direct sun, or a full day of very bright shade, this rose will perform quite respectably. If the natural shape of the bush is too large for your garden, 'Ballerina' can be trained onto a fence or trellis.

BALTIMORE BELLE
Hybrid Setigera. Introduced 1843.

The Irish have a word for a day when the mist is more luxurious than usual, a day when you feel enveloped by the climate that keeps their hills so green. They call it a "soft" day, and 'Baltimore Belle' is what you might, with the same idea in mind, call a "soft" rose. The clusters of double flowers are blush pale, with delicate petals full of fragrance. They hang in washes from long canes covered with equally soft green leaves. The rose only blooms in the late spring, just about the right time to carry on a courtship under its influence.

This is obviously a romantic rose, but also a good subject for training. It's breeding is assumed to be the Prairie Rose, our native roadside beauty *R. setigera*, crossed with one of the Noisettes. 'Baltimore Belle' will climb from 8 to 12 feet, depending on the severity of winters, and the canes are flexible, not too thorny. On the other hand, it's subject to some blackspot, even the occasional case of rust, after the bloom season. This rose actually prefers a little shade if air circulation is good, and works best on a fence where it can perform at peak and then be masked a little by later garden flowers. It's often grown on arbors in spite of potential drawbacks— it is just good, sometimes, to be surrounded by softness.

BARONNE PRÉVOST
Hybrid Perpetual. Introduced 1842.

A good shrub and a sturdy one, 'Baronne Prévost' combines a controlled and upright form like that of 'Marchesa Boccella' with huge pink flowers like those of 'Paul Neyron'. It is not quite as memorable as either of these other two Hybrid Perpetuals, but it is even more serviceable in the garden. The bush is about 4 feet tall and 3 wide, smaller than 'Marchesa Boccella', with thick, slightly coarse foliage. The wide flat flowers are very double and very fragrant, not quite as large as those of 'Paul Neyron', but produced much more freely. Their strong pink color stands out well against the leaves, and they last a good long time when used in a cut flower arrangement.

'Baronne Prévost' can be fit easily into most garden designs, even grown in a container, and has less trouble with fungus diseases than most others of its class. It will thrive on good soil and regular care, tolerating both cold and hot climates with little difficulty. If you want to try a classic Old Garden Rose in with a group of Hybrid Teas, this variety's erect form will blend in visually with the modern roses. It can even be pruned like a Hybrid Tea, though moderate pruning will bring just as many flowers.

BASYE'S BLUEBERRY
Shrub. Introduced 1982.

Although created with deliberate awareness in Dr. Robert Basye's program to breed roses that are blackspot free, this rose presents a flower of blushing innocence. Each set of deep pink, richly fragrant, wide-open petals is dominated by a huge circle of golden stamens. The effect is somehow big-eyed, like an eager young thing looking upon the world with amazement and approval. The flowers fold up quietly every night and gradually fade with exposure, falling off after only three days. The innocence is heightened by a near absence of thorns, another breeding criterion of Dr. Basye. The actual name comes from the resemblance of the plant, with its upright canes and neatly rounded leaves, to a large and vigorous blueberry bush.

For all its simple charm, 'Basye's Blueberry' is far from delicate. It will reach a good 6 feet in height in just a few years, and it seems to thrive in the typical clay soils and alkaline water of its native Texas. This rose is an excellent subject for hedging, easy to clip because of the few prickles and constantly in bloom through the growing season. Its simple semi-double flowers and tidy leaves are little affected by the worst heat of summer, and as an extra treat you get very round, shiny orange hips and foliage that changes color in the fall.

BASYE'S PURPLE
Hybrid Rugosa. Introduced 1968.

As a child, all shades of purple were my favorite color. Age has brought sophistication, but the velvety petals of this rose satisfy an unforgotten longing for seriously purple things. I can't believe that any blue rose breeders may produce in the future could be as rewarding. 'Basye's Purple' is more than just the one color, of course. The five-petaled flowers are crowned with circlets of old-gold stamens and produced in clusters set on platforms of rough but shapely green leaves that turn rusty orange in the autumn. These clusters are held up by thick and thorny canes the color of burgundy wine. The parent roses were *R. rugosa* and *R. foliosa*, and the result is an entire plant that looks like no other rose in the garden.

'Basye's Purple' shows rugosa heritage both in a clove-based fragrance and in a tendency to increase by throwing up occasional suckers from the roots. These suckers can be left in place if desired, because otherwise the bush will never expand very much in width, or they can be shovel pruned to keep the narrow, upright form intact. It's a very healthy rose, better adapted to heavy soils than many other hybrid rugosas. The biggest challenge is in pruning: it seems a shame to cut back the beautiful canes, but left unchecked in a good organic soil they can reach up to 7 feet in height with flower clusters almost out of reach. This fascinating rose may not be exactly what Dr. Basye planned when selecting for thornlessness, but it is definitely a work of art.

BELINDA
Hybrid Musk. Introduced 1936.

Of all the varieties created under the Hybrid Musk classification, none is more gifted than this rose at combining beauty and utility. The heavy clusters of hot pink, semi-double flowers are compelling when seen from a distance. Up close, the white eye and bright stamens add to the delicacy of each blossom's individual charm. The only drawback to the flowers themselves is a lack of strong fragrance, though there is a light perfume when conditions are right.

'Belinda' is naturally a moderate climber, with prickly but flexible canes covered with neat, disease resistant foliage for most of their 10 foot length. Spread out on a trellis it can function as a blanket of color whenever it blooms, but the convenient size also allows it to be used as a more conservative focal point by winding it around a single pillar. It can also be allowed to grow free-form in a casually sprawling shape, with the flower clusters so weighting the mature branches that the bush will be much wider than it is tall. I have seen it used by more than one gardener as a hedge, pruned from 3 to 4 feet high. Willing as ever, 'Belinda' performed beautifully in this situation, even thriving on the hard pruning and putting on constant moderate displays all summer and outrageous productions in spring and fall.

BELINDA'S DREAM
Shrub. Introduced 1988.

Dr. Robert Basye has always felt that if he could just grow the perfect thornless, blackspot free bush, someone else could breed pretty flowers onto it. We all have weaknesses, however, and when 'Belinda's Dream' developed in his test garden he allowed it to be introduced with the name of the young daughter of some close friends. It is far from meeting his high standards of perfection, for it does have good strong thorns widely spaced along the stiff canes. The bush is very disease resistant, however, and though Dr. Basye didn't select specifically for this, it happens to have gorgeous flowers.

One parent, the old Hybrid Tea 'Tiffany', won a number of prestigious awards, including the medal for fragrance. The other parent was 'Jersey Beauty', a once-blooming climber bred from *R. wichuraiana* and the great yellow Tea rose 'Perle des Jardins'. 'Belinda's Dream' is a fine clean pink, fat, double, and high-centered rose in the classic Hybrid Tea style. It makes a great cut flower as well as a good garden rose, and is a perfect gift for someone ready to widen their rose horizons, but not yet willing to branch out too far. The bush is a moderate size, able to reach 6 feet but usually maintaining at about 4 feet high by 3 wide. The canes will occasionally show some dieback, but this is a grooming problem, not a disease problem, and is easy to keep controlled.

BELLE STORY
Shrub. Introduced 1985.

The original Belle Story was a nurse who became an officer in the British Royal Navy—she must have been a lovely person if her rose is representative of her character. Large, double flowers of pale pink are slightly cupped around a broad circle of bright yellow stamens. The stamens turn reddish very quickly, so the rose seems to have a large dark eye even though the petals are really pale gold at the base. The fragrance is very rich and lingers even when the flowers have been cut and brought indoors. 'Belle' is a big bush, easily reaching 5 feet in height and 4 feet across, so it makes a good backdrop for shorter roses both old and modern. The canes are sturdy and erect, reminiscent of the Floribunda 'Iceberg' that is one of the parents, and the neat mid-green foliage is slightly glossy. Like most of the other David Austin introductions, this rose will do beautifully in some locations and not so well in others—his English roses are just as much individuals as any other group of varieties with widely varied genes. 'Belle Story' has flowers that tolerate heat and humidity well, even if the foliage occasionally suffers from blackspot in the warmth of the South. A little afternoon shade will help keep the rose at its leafy best.

BISHOP DARLINGTON
Hybrid Musk. Introduced 1926.

The classic practice of naming roses for people can't help but lead to odd questions now and then. Who was the original Bishop Darlington, and why, exactly, does this rose carry his name? It's a fine and handsome bush, impressive in its large (up to 8 feet tall by 4 feet wide) and rigidly erect posture. But it is scantily clad. The foliage is attractive but sparse—if it were clothing, one might say it was wearing just enough to suggest it could all come off. The open, semi-double flowers are equally coy, with their perfumed silken petals of pale peach and creamy pink. One petal is always curled over the exposed golden stamens, just as the hands of Venus, in so many statues, call attention to what they pretend to hide. But enough: 'Bishop Darlington' is a very pretty rose and a very useful shrub. It can be kept pruned to a height of about 5 feet, so that the large pale flowers fill in the gap between shorter flowering plants and climbers overhead. It will make a sturdy hedge, or, left to itself, mound up quite tall into an outstanding specimen to fill a large space, against a barn wall for example. The hips are large, held as stiffly upright as the flowers that precede them. This rose blooms well even in the heat of August and makes a good cut flower.

BLANC DOUBLE DE COUBERT
Hybrid Rugosa. Introduced 1892.

In the heat of summer the only time to be outside is early morning or in the evening, and when the light is low it's the pale colors that reign supreme in the garden. 'Blanc Double de Coubert' shines at these times, with large semi-double flowers

of crinkled, spice-scented white silk. The rough leaves are a rich green backdrop to roses whose fragrance lingers even at night or in cool weather, and to the successive crops of orangey hips.

'Blanc Double de Coubert' is a good rugosa for the upper South, performing well into the top half of zone 8. It has some Tea blood from one of its parents, 'Sombreuil', to help it tolerate heat and clay-cramped roots. As with almost all the rugosas, however, it will reach its mature size (5 feet high by 4 wide) more rapidly if planted in a light, sand-and-gypsum-amended soil. Disease is not much of a problem, as long as drainage is good, but it will put up new starts from root suckers. Afternoon shade for added coolness is not only tolerated but preferred, and any shadows will be brightened by the whiteness of the flowers.

BLAZE
Large-flowered Climber. Introduced 1932.

You can buy it at Wal-Mart, you can see it straggling along institutional chain link fences, almost everybody on the poor side of town has one sitting out in their yard with or without a little bed and a nice white tire. 'Blaze' is everywhere, oddly used and oddly pruned, and as often an eyesore as a sight for sore eyes, but for all that it's a great rose. Impeccable breeding ('Paul's Scarlet Climber' x 'Gruss an Teplitz', with 'Rêve d'Or' as a grandparent) combined with amazing toughness have allowed it to survive and bloom in situations that would appall the Society for Prevention of Cruelty to Roses—if there were one. The flowers are a distinctive shade of medium red that can be identified from a distance, a good plain color that anyone could be comfortable with. They are medium sized and semi-double, but cupped, so they look fuller, and borne in clusters, so they look larger. The fragrance is light, but the bloom is constant, with the best shows in the spring and autumn months. 'Blaze' is a moderate climber, in the 8- to 12- foot range, with strong but flexible canes and plenty of dark foliage—when it's gotten enough care to have any foliage at all. It can, obviously, survive almost any condition, but when treated well it is not only reliable but gorgeous. Don't be put off because everyone has one: everyone should.

BLUE MIST
Miniature. Introduced 1970.

Those who were born before 1970—I think there are still a few of us—will be interested to know that what seems such a recent rose has already been "lost" and rediscovered. Though still available commercially, this same rose (near as I can tell from growing them side by side) is offered by a local nursery as a "found" variety under a temporary study name. The found plant will probably soon be definitely identified—easier to do with a recent introduction than a very old variety—but it's interesting that someone saw it in a garden and liked it enough to collect it simply on its own merits.

'Blue Mist' is a nifty little rounded bush with plenty of healthy light green leaves and clusters of soft mauve pink blossoms. The individual flowers are double, but they open fully to show their tiny yellow stamens and release their pleasant spicy perfume. Though classified as a micro-mini, the bush reaches 2 or 3 feet in every direction in the long Southern growing season and is remarkably versatile in the garden. It can be used in containers, under taller roses to fill them out, or even clipped into a loose border for herb garden beds, where a row of plants in bloom would indeed seem to be covered with a soft mist of color.

BLUSH NOISETTE
Noisette. Introduced 1817.

The original 'Blush Noisette' was a seedling of the famous 'Champneys' Pink Cluster', the first rose known to be bred in America. Philippe, a Charleston horticulturist, worked with his nurseryman brother Louis in France to develop the Noisette line of China/Musk crosses into fragrant, repeat blooming garden roses that bore their name. Unfortunately, there's no way to know whether we still have the original 'Blush Noisette' that the Noisette brothers selected. 'Champneys' Pink Cluster' seems to have been outstandingly fertile as a seed parent, because the South is thickly populated today with variations on the

early Noisette theme. The 'Blush Noisette' available in commerce today is very similar to old paintings, however, so unless you're a genetic perfectionist you should be very happy with it. It's more compact, with better foliage and more blackspot resistance than its seed parent, and it has larger, more strongly colored flowers whose clusters still carry the deliciously strong Noisette fragrance. The blossoms are cupped and semi-double, blush white in the summer and soft rose pink when the weather is cool, very delicate and romantic in appearance. The bush can reach up to 7 feet, but is more commonly seen about 4½ feet high and 3 wide, just right for a herb garden, fragrance garden, or container.

BOULE DE NEIGE
Bourbon. Introduced 1867.

Of three seed sisters, 'Boule de Niege' ("Ball of Snow") is the only one to have flowers of pure white. Both 'Coquette des Alpes' and 'Coquette des Blanches', also resulting from the cross of 'Blanche Lafitte' (a Bourbon) and 'Sappho' (a Tea), have a pink tinge. Nothing wrong with a pink tinge, but the odd sister out also seems to repeat its blooming a little more often, and if you can only find space for one of these, that's a deciding factor for a long growing season. Midsummer may bring some blackspot and scanty blossoms, but overall the rose does very well in the South. The flowers are deliciously fat with

petals, stone white, rounded, and very fragrant. In areas of very high humidity or constant rainfall they may have trouble with balling, but it's a price rose gardeners have always had to pay for loving this kind of floral decadence. The bush can get very large, up to 6 feet tall and eventually as wide. The flexible canes droop over under the weight of dark green foliage and snowball blossoms, which means 'Boule de Niege' is a good candidate as a pillar or pegged rose, though I've seen it most often tangled with other roses at the back of a large border.

BUFF BEAUTY
Hybrid Musk. Introduced 1939.
Elizabeth Winston, founder of The Organic Plant Institute, has claimed this as her favorite rose out of a collection of some three hundred. She's a woman gifted with both good sense and good taste, so her choice has never disappointed her. 'Buff Beauty' is a sturdy, healthy climber with canes reaching up to a comfortable 12 feet, just long enough to be braided up a pillar or trained on an arch so the unique flowers will start about face height. This is important because of the strong sweet fragrance, a result of breeding that's really only about one quarter Hybrid Musk to three quarters Tea-Noisette. Being physically close to the flowers is also nice because the medium-sized double blossoms are an unusual buff apricot color, great to cut for indoor arrangements with crimson roses. 'Buff Beauty', like some of the other Hybrid Musks, may go a little short of foliage in midsummer, but its only real drawback as a climber is a tendency to throw out rigid, short branching canes as well as long, easily trained ones. These can be pruned off, or the rose can be grown as a large shrub with no supports if there's enough garden space. Hips on this variety make a reliable display from late summer well into the winter.

CALDWELL PINK
"Found" Polyantha. No date of introduction known.
This rose was collected in Caldwell, Texas, and its flowers are pink. Other than that, the proper identification is a mystery. It isn't exactly like others of its tentative classification, in that it goes dormant in the late fall (after shedding a fine display of rusty orange foliage) and comes out of dormancy late in the spring, keeping its canes cautiously bare while Chinas, Teas, and other Polyanthas are already in full bloom. It *is* like the others somewhat in the foliage and blossom characteristics, and in being an almost indestructible plant with almost continuous bloom (once it gets started). It may very well be an old and forgotten Polyantha, or even perhaps a Floribunda, or the dwarf sport of an old Rambler—a similar climbing rose has been found as well. "Caldwell Pink" is such a good landscape plant we may as well memorize it under the study name, because if it's ever identified it'll be impossible to go back and correct the tags on all the thousands of plants already sold. The flowers are very double, medium-sized muddled pompoms with an old rose look to them, though they have no fragrance. They are borne freely on a well-branched, stiff bush about 3 feet high and wide. The foliage is soft-looking rather than glossy, which adds

to the old rose appearance. Disease resistance is excellent; I've seen powdery mildew develop when 'Caldwell Pink' was planted in damp shade, but that might happen to anybody. In the sun it's not only trouble free, it's almost maintenance free. Whatever it is, there should be more like it.

CAREFREE WONDER
Shrub. Introduced 1990.

A lot of people really like this rose and look to it as a signpost of good things to come in the garden. 'Carefree Wonder' is the result of crossing American breeder Griffith Buck's 'Prairie Princess', known for cold hardiness and disease tolerance, with a number of more modern roses. This rose is actually intercontinental: it was bred in France (by the Meilland firm that's making a name for themselves with disease-resistant roses to fill new niches in the garden), where it's been grown since 1978. Once it finally got registered and introduced in the States, it gained immediate popularity.

Like its sturdy grandparent, 'Carefree Wonder' is extremely resistant to powdery mildew and fairly resistant to blackspot. It's a very free bloomer, with a tolerance for both heat and cold. The flowers are large, double, and fairly open so that the pale yellow and red-streaked stamens show in the white center. The medium pink petals that have a pale pink reverse and a strong Tea fragrance when they first open. There's plenty of foliage on the prickly canes, with reddish new growth and distinctive, deeply serrated edges to the leaflets that make the plant easy to recognize at a distance. 'Carefree Wonder' has a bushy 4-foot high by 3-foot wide build that makes it perfect for hedging. It also offers a crop of hips to entice wildlife and is low-maintenance enough to plant at the wild edges of the garden.

CÉCILE BRUNNER
Polyantha. Introduced 1881.

In colder climates this rose probably grows as a cute little bush to complement the perfectly formed, high-centered, warm pink miniature·buds that long ago got it christened "The Sweetheart Rose." Mild winters allow the same plant to easily reach heights of 4 or 5 feet (a heavier-blooming form, 'Spray Cécile Brunner', can double that size), while hot summers load it with awkwardly thrust-out clusters of small, sun-bleached flesh-colored blooms—it is a favorite Southern heirloom all the same. It does get some blackspot, but it's so adaptable that leaving it off the list of really tough roses would be ridiculous. It

will grow in any garden conditions, even non-garden conditions. Having noted that, I must say I personally prefer the climbing sport introduced in 1894. That has the same dainty spice-scented flowers, which really are pretty in the cool of spring and fall, and I find them more attractive scattered along a graceful cane. 'Cécile Brunner, Climbing' is remarkably vigorous, one of those plants that's almost sentient in its ability to expand and defend its territory. It will tolerate any kind of soil, grow 20 feet into shade trees, cross fences to annex a neighbor's yard, and survive all kinds of neglect.

It's handsomer, of course, if cared for, but that can be a tricky chore. This rose, both as a bush and a climber, has strongly curved, wickedly sharp thorns and an apparent desire to utilize the nitrogen of human blood. The climber has the advantage of height and flexible canes when attacking, but the bush shouldn't be underestimated. However you choose to enjoy the charming flowers, you'll probably pay for it—and probably grow deeply attached to the Sweetheart Rose just the same.

CELSIANA
Damask. Introduced before 1750.

Whoever came up with the idea that the world looked better through rose-colored glasses must have been familiar with a rose like 'Celsiana'. The wide, semi-double flowers have petals of the palest translucent pink; you can't really see through their fragrant folds, but the effect is not unlike light through a stained glass window of the most delicate beauty. Add to this the Damask perfume (which always makes me wish I could bathe in it, or roll in it, or somehow get it all over me permanently) and you have a very uplifting experience. As an old European vari-ety, 'Celsiana' only blooms once during the growing sea-son, so you never grow jaded with its beauty or let down by seeing these exquisite flowers looking ratty in the summer heat. The grey-green leaves make a perfect set-ting for this particular shade of pink, and the 4- to 5-foot canes, with only a light sprinkling of prickles, are firm enough to hold the flowers up to the light while flex-ible enough to train on a pillar or trellis.

'Celsiana' is not disease prone, but constant heat and hard soils together can diminish its natural resistance until it sheds itself bald in the summer. With a well-pre-pared, well-drained organic bed and plenty of mulch and water, this is quite a sound variety for representing its class in the South. In zone 7 and north it should be even more sturdy, though it couldn't possibly be more beautiful.

CHEROKEE ROSE, *Rosa laevigata*
Species. Introduced 1759.

This rose has a history so entwined with Southern tradition it would be impos-sible to untangle it at this late date. A native of China, it's been naturalized here so long it was adopted as the state flower of Georgia. Folk legend says it was carried by the Cherokee Indians as they left their southeastern homelands on the Trail of Tears to Oklahoma, and that they planted cuttings of it along the way. The spread is much more attributable to nurseryman Thomas Affleck, of Mississippi and Texas, who rec-ommended and sold mass quantities of this rose as one of the best possible hedge plants for a plantation, before the invention of barbed wire. It's often confused with another naturalized Chinese rose, the Macartney Rose (*R. bracteata*), which has become a major agricultural pest in the deep South by spreading so freely from seed and sucker. This latter rose does have a similar five-petaled white flower, but it's not only distinctly different in its botanical parts, it blooms in the summer while the "Cherokee Rose" blooms only in early spring. I know at least one town that insists on having a Cherokee Rose Festival while the Macartney menace is in full flower—there are probably many more instances of the two species' total confusion. (A new pink Hybrid Tea has recently been registered as 'The McCartney Rose', to add to the confusion.) *Rosa laevigata* is a lovely and vigorous climber (but not invasive!) to 15 feet or more, with leaves consisting of three glossy green leaflets decorating its individually-carried large, fragrant, white flowers. It occasionally produces hips, but doesn't appear to self-start from them. This rose is a good one to cover an ugly shed or soften a large section of fence (or *be* a large section of fence) with its handsome glossy foliage and eye-catching spring flowers.

CHESTNUT ROSE, *Rosa roxburghii*
Species. Introduced before 1814.

The common name refers to both the buds and the hips (though this rose rarely sets fruit below zone 8), which are covered with chestnut-burr-like prickles. This characteristic has also earned it the name "Chinquapin Rose," and, although the prickles are not soft or scented, "Moss Rose." It's under the latter name that I've run across it most often, probably because true Moss roses are hard to keep going in the deep South and there's nothing with which to compare it. Originally introduced from China, the Chestnut Rose is a staple of old Southern gardens: you can pretty much assume every time someone tells you their mother has a Moss rose, they mean this.

In addition to prickly buds, which open to very double lilac pink flowers of old-fashioned beauty but no fragrance, the Chestnut Rose has odd, grey-brown peeling bark and long delicate leaves comprised of up to 15 leaflets. Unlike many species, there is quite often some repeat bloom after the initial cascading burst. It grows in a naturally arching form that can reach 7 feet high and wide, but the tendency to plant it in the shade (or maybe the magnolias just grow up around it over the decades) often keeps it much smaller. It's a very healthy and long-lived plant, with some specimens probably dating to before the Civil War.

CINDERELLA
Miniature. Introduced 1953.

This micro-mini is a jewel and perfectly named, for the rose is both magically pretty and capable of the hard work of daily life. It's the perfect little girl's rose: my niece, Angela, who's just reached double digits in age, has enjoyed it for several years now. Her plant has survived in the same small pot with haphazard care and imperfect lighting, still producing its tiny and very double satiny pale pink flowers on a regular basis. Their spicy scent is quite strong for a Miniature, much appreciated in a class whose members aren't known for fragrance. In addition to its obvious toughness and tenacity, 'Cinderella' is almost without prickles—safe for nieces and very pleasant to work with in any garden situation. The little plant barely reaches 2 feet high, even in a well-maintained bed, so it's a good idea to cluster several together if you want it to be noticed. The color, which fades nearly white in the sun, is a paler echo of roses such as 'Souvenir de la Malmaison', so the plants can be used to fill in with soft color near that rather awkwardly open shrub. 'Cinderella' also can be kept as a dainty pot plant for a small niche, or used with a combination of other plants in a larger container.

CLOTILDE SOUPERT
Polyantha. Introduced 1890.

I received a letter from a lady in her 80's, telling me she had a beautiful rose her grandmother had grown and asking for identification. It didn't matter if it was blooming when I came, she wrote, because she'd painted it last fall when the weather was cool and the color was strongest, and she was sure she'd captured it perfectly. At her house a few weeks later she showed me the painting before she showed me the plant. I hadn't realized how very distinctive the color and form of 'Clotilde Soupert' really are: I instantly recognized the amazingly double cream pink flowers with their deep pink center blush and their neatly cupped tissue-paper thin petals. The flowers are very large for a Polyantha, as big as those of a full-sized Tea rose, and often produced in clusters of three or more, as she'd painted them. The bush nestled against her tool shed had the typical full shape, about 3½ feet high and nearly as wide, and the light green foliage normal to 'Clotilde Soupert' in an alkaline soil—it does "canary in the gold mine" duty for chlorosis, though that doesn't seem to affect either growth or blooming. In a container or in well-maintained soil the nearly thornless plant is very lush and handsome. My new friend affirmed that the very fragrant flowers tended to ball in wet weather and occasionally got powdery mildew, but that it didn't matter because new flowers were always on the way. We parted in mutual satisfaction, agreeing that it was a very good rose indeed and that she'd done a fine job with the painting. There is also a climbing form of this rose that is equally floriferous and will grow vigorously to 12 or 15 feet.

COMTESSE DU CAYLA
China. Introduced 1902.

Silk is a wonderful fabric, not just because of the sheer elegance of its texture but because of the way it reflects light, often seeming to glow with two or more colors at once. Certain roses capture this quality in their petals, and 'Comtesse du Cayla' is one of them. The slightly cupped, semi-double flowers are orangey red, washed with a pale golden peach that seems like a reflection of the golden stamens in the open centers. The canes are dark, almost burgundy, with a red tint to the newest leaves as well that accents the blossoms beautifully. The sweet fruity China fragrance is very strong in the flowers, with a peppery scent to the sepals just under the buds. 'Comtesse du Cayla' is a very versatile plant, bushy and vigorous to about 3 feet in every direction. Its handy size makes it useful to plant in containers and small beds, such as herb gardens, as well as mixed into larger borders. It has the tolerance of all China roses for devastating heat and humidity combined with alkaline water, but it will perform best when given a reasonable soil and some drainage. When using it in garden design remember that the majority of the flowers will be borne on shoots thrust slightly above the surface of the bush, so the overall effect is open and airy rather than dense and compact.

CONSTANCE SPRY
Shrub. Introduced 1961.

This is the earliest of David Austin's fascinating group of roses, and it sets a standard of beauty upon which later varieties can hardly improve. 'Constance Spry' only blooms once a year, but it's more than worth the wait. The enormous, very double rich pink flowers are cupped like chalices and filled to the rim with an extraordinary fragrance, which Austin describes as "myrrh." If this is what myrrh smells like, then it's easy to see why it would be a gift for a king and used to ease the sorrows of the dying—it's wonderful. The plant that bears these terrific flowers is handsome as well, but not easy to fit into every garden. The breeding includes the old Gallica, 'Belle Isis', and the long slender canes—which have plenty of narrow prickles to break off in your fingers while grooming—grow in a whiplike, more-or-less upright Gallica style to a height of 7 feet or more. This is in warm climates, where the plant is a little stressed. In England it seems to reach a mature height of more than 15 feet, becoming a true climber. 'Constance Spry' does have a preference for cool weather and may hold back on blooming if it doesn't get adequate chilling hours, so it's probably not a good choice below zone 8. If you can offer it the right weather and can find room for it—on a pillar or tripod, pegged, trellised, or even left to weave itself through other large shrubs in the back of the border—its magnificent flowers will make you feel that you've arrived as a gardener and have, by god, produced some ROSES.

CORNELIA
Hybrid Musk. Introduced 1925.

Reverend Pemberton had the same idea as David Austin: breed garden-worthy roses from a combination of old and new varieties. The difference is that Pemberton seems to have preferred the visual effect of smaller flowers in large clusters, on plants that would perform as either large shrubs or vigorous climbers. 'Cornelia' is one of the finest of this type, bearing masses of small strawberry and copper double flowers on thickly foliaged canes that can reach up to 12 feet in length. The fragrance is moderate, a musky scent easier to detect under some conditions than others, but the floral display in spring and again in fall is outstanding, and there are almost always a few clusters of blossoms throughout the growing season. 'Cornelia's' natural form is arched and spreading, with the heavy canes pulling the shrub much wider than it is tall. Left to grow in this habit it makes an outstanding specimen, especially cascading over low walls or down a bank into a water feature. The only real pruning needed is periodic thinning of any canes that spoil the arching form. As a climber, 'Cornelia' is easiest to train when young and flexible, so if it is to be a pillar or trellis rose it's a good idea to start early. This rose tolerates a good deal of bright shade and doesn't mind alkaline soils.

lis. Lots of new canes are produced every year once 'Danaë' is about three years old, so if space is confined it's a good idea to thin out a number of the oldest canes during spring pruning: about ⅓ of the total is the general rule of thumb. If, on the other hand, you have a lot of room to fill up, this rose can be left unsupported to mound up as a shrub at least 5 feet high and wide. It tolerates shade very well, needing only a few hours of direct sun to stay healthy and blooming.

DICK KOSTER
Polyantha. Introduced 1929.

Who needs breeders to get new roses? 'Dick Koster' is the centerpiece of a basket full of sports, new cultivars created by the tendency of certain roses to throw out a shoot (which can be used for propagation) differing from the type in flower color or number of petals or climbing habit or dwarfism. Some roses never do this, while others have produced numerous new varieties with little apparent effort. The "Koster" family line goes back to the Hybrid Multiflora 'Tausendschön'. That rose sported 'Echo' in 1914, a compact form of itself still classed as a Hybrid Multiflora. 'Echo' sported 'Greta Kluis' in 1916, changing the color from pink and white to carmine red, and the class designation to Polyantha. From that came 'Anneke Koster' (deep red) in 1927, which sported our rose. From 'Dick Koster' alone sprang 'Margo Koster' (salmon) in 1931, 'Mothersday' (dark pink) in 1949, 'Dick Koster Superior' (rosy red) in 1955, and 'Margo Koster Superior' (deep salmon pink) in 1956. Those are just the ones I happen to know about, without mentioning at least two further sports from 'Margo Koster', one as recent as 1987.

These are all wonderful compact roses, healthy and floriferous. 'Dick Koster's' flowers are representative of its whole group of descendants, borne in clusters of round little buds that open to very cupped, dark pink blossoms with no fragrance but great visual appeal and terrific lasting qualities. They can ball in wet weather, but the plant keeps on blooming so the lost flowers are negligible. The leaves are also small, glossy, and very disease resistant on a bush that stays 2 to 3 feet in height. 'Dick Koster' is a truly useful rose in the landscape or in containers; it's very convenient to have it recreated in a selection of colors.

DOG ROSE, *Rosa canina*
Species. Cultivated before 1737.

This large Species rose is not meant as a formal garden plant, though it is one of the prettiest wild roses to bloom in hedgerows in the spring, both in its native Europe and in areas of the United States where it has naturalized. It was used for a long time as a favorite understock, so many specimens can be found where the grafted rose died away and left the tough support system behind. *R. canina* is a common sight in older California cemeteries. The single, light pink to near-white flowers with delicately separated petals are produced late in the spring blooming season, covering the mounding shrub like a flight of pale butterflies. The flowers are followed by a wonderful crop of dark orange, shiny hips—to me, this is the main reason for growing the plant. Seventeenth-century horticulturist John Gerard even refers to this rose as "The Hep Tree." Dog Rose hips are still the variety most commonly sold for culinary purposes, and they're very tasty in any recipe.

The plant is a big twiggy bush, not unlike the Eglantine rose in form. *R. Eglanteria* is a closely related species with fragrant foliage. It is usually a 6- or 7-foot-high-and-wide mound of tangled canes but it can reach 10 feet or more quite easily, displaying its glossy leaves and curved prickles (there is a thornless variety) as an awkward climber. This rose is native to cold climates, so it does very well from upper zone 8 northward. The Dog Rose can be more difficult to keep going in the deep South, but if you have a lightly shaded spot at the edge of some piney woods, you may want to try naturalizing it. Birds will be grateful for the protected nesting site, and any hips you don't want will be very welcome on their winter menu.

DON JUAN
Large-flowered Climber. Introduced 1958.

Living up to the reputation of the legendary Latin lover, 'Don Juan' prefers warm climates and has climbed many a Southern wall to steal rose lovers' hearts. It also continues to win at rose shows. The variety was introduced to fill a niche for Hybrid Tea-type blossoms on a repeat-blooming climbing plant. The double, richly fragrant flowers are so deep red that the buds are almost black. They open from high centers and gradually spread out into wide cups, 4 or 5 inches across, in a slow process that makes them excellent long-lasting cut flowers. 'Don Juan' is not a huge plant—the canes rarely reach more than 10 feet in length—so it makes a good subject for pillars or smaller spaces where a distinctive climbing rose is desirable. I pruned one specimen into a 3-foot-tall shrub for lack of climbing space, and was pleased to find it made a very cooperative bush. The flowers are produced not in large flushes but with remarkable constancy from early spring until after the first frosts, with the fall flowers being the largest and most intense in color. Dead-heading will keep the bloom cycle stimulated, but you may want to leave a few spent flowers alone because 'Don Juan' also produces fat and dramatic orange hips.

DORTMUND
Kordesii. Introduced 1955.

'Dortmund' demands attention, both because of its fire-engine red color and because the light, wavy petals grouped in masses suggest a migration of hot butterflies on the verge of departure. The flowers are registered as single, but they often have as many as eight lightly fragrant petals opening more or less flat from a white eye. It's a hybrid of the manmade Species rose *R. kordesii*, which passed on the ability to set tasty hips in abundance, plus the oddly shaped, dark green and deeply serrated foliage. It also has inherited the vigor and disease resistance of the wild roses (*R. wichuraiana* and *R. rugosa*) whose interbreeding started the new Kordesii strain.

'Dortmund' is great in the landscape because it can be so eye-catchingly colorful when covered with masses of bloom and yet look graceful and attractive when it's between cycles and just shows a few blossoms. The only time it doesn't look good is when it's grown in too much shade and gets temporarily defoliated by fungus; it needs at least 6 hours of good sun. The canes normally reach about 10 or 12 feet in length once the plant is established—though they can grow up to 20 feet in an ideal situation—and they can be trained on any support available. 'Dortmund' has the gift of decorating even a tacky building or bad paint job so that the whole thing looks like a conscious artistic choice.

DOUBLE DELIGHT
Hybrid Tea. Introduced 1977.

Winner of several international medals—one for fragrance—and countless exhibition prizes, 'Double Delight' has remained a garden favorite since its introduction some twenty years ago. The striking flowers are double, very large and high-centered (sometimes double-centered), with cream white petals edged with strawberry when first opening. After several days' exposure to sun, the spicy-scented blossoms blush strawberry red all over. (Grown in the greenhouse with no ultraviolet light, the flowers remain pure white.) The plant is only a moderate 3 to 4 feet in height, but all the same this rose isn't one to blend tamely into the landscape. You can count on it to be a focal point, so make sure you plant it or set it in a container at a place where you'll frequently want to look. One of the nicest uses I've seen so far was a planting of three 'Double Delight' roses accented on one side by a clump of 'Maurine Neuberger' red Miniature roses and on the other by a mound of silvery artemisia.

This rose is fairly bushy for a Hybrid Tea, with foliage that remains in good shape through most pitfalls of the growing season. In heavy shade or cool dry weather, however, there may be a temporary bout of powdery mildew, which is easily treatable with a brisk foliage wash or baking soda spray (see p. 72). The handsome, slow-opening flowers are as valuable in cut arrangements for the home as they are for the exhibition table.

DUCHER
China. Introduced 1869.

Cool and handsome, 'Ducher' looks like snow in a pine forest. The medium-sized flowers have petals of pure white, though the light reflected between them can take on a creamy lemon tone. The rose is very double, almost Tea-like, but with the fruity sweet scent characteristic of the most fragrant Chinas. Unlike many white roses, the petals of this unique variety (it's the only white China still in commerce) drop fairly cleanly when spent and don't linger forever on the bush, turning brown and ugly. The foliage is dark green, with burgundy new growth, and those two deep colors make a wonderful backdrop for the balls of white. The compact, bushy plant reaches 3 to 4 feet in height by about 2 to 3 feet wide, and works for containers, low hedges, or any mixture of plants in a border. 'Ducher' is an excellent choice for blending some of the rather rigid modern large-flowered roses with more delicate old varieties in the garden through its combination of crisp color and the soft fullness of its flowers and foliage. It's a very healthy variety, tolerating heat, sun, bad water, and worse soil—as if to the Southland born.

DUCHESSE DE BRABANT
Tea. Introduced 1857.

Nearly every description of this rose mentions the fact that it was President Theodore Roosevelt's favorite variety and that he often wore it in his buttonhole (according to a letter from his widow printed in an American Rose Society annual). Surely, in nearly a century and a half, someone else has liked it as well? Everyone that I know certainly does. The large, double, cupped pink flowers look just like the luxurious roses spilling about in old paintings, and the fragrance is both reliable and intense. This is a rose you can count on being able to smell at any time of day or night, under any conditions, no matter how bad your allergies get. The scent is the essence of Tea: a strong, dry, slightly acrid sweetness that is very memorable and nothing like the commercial perfume sold under that name. The flowers and fragrance are supported by a handsome, vase-shaped bush that averages about 4 feet in height and at least 3 across. The foliage is generous, with leaves of mild green that are slightly wavy—a characteristic of only a few specific Tea varieties. 'Duchesse de Brabant' is a healthy, beautiful, and easy rose, one of the best for a nervous beginner to rose gardening, or as a present for someone you really need to please.

EGLANTINE, *Rosa eglanteria*
Species. Introduced before 1551.

Growing a rose of this antiquity is not unlike holding a lump of amber containing a mosquito fed on the blood of dinosaurs; you can't help but sense the history if you have any imagination at all. Of course, you may want to grow "Eglantine" even if you have zero interest in antiquity or literature: it makes the whole garden smell good. Closely related to the Dog rose, this wild rose only blooms in the spring, but it's not the rosy scent of the small, single pink flowers that matters. The foliage itself is perfumed with the breeze-borne sweet aroma of sweet green apples, and every time the sprinkler or a rain shower wets the leaves, a cloud of fruity fragrance can be smelled yards away. It was this attribute that led to its common name of "sweet briar."

Eglantine is not a plant for a small space. Pruned as a shrub, it will be comfortably 6 or 7 feet tall and nearly as wide. It can also be trained as a rough climber to about 12 feet, by anyone who doesn't mind handling the canes full of truly vicious prickles. There's no point trying to make it be little: hard pruning will result in no flowers until it's grown back to a size it likes. As the centerpiece of a large herb garden, or the backdrop for a scented border, it is unequaled. In the warmest zones this rose is apt to shed some foliage in the summer, and it's susceptible to rust now and then. Good mulch and regular root zone watering in well-drained soil will keep it more attractive until cool weather restores it to beauty. If the spring bloom was good, a crop of prickly but flavorful orange hips will follow.

ELSE POULSEN
Floribunda. Introduced 1924.

'Else Poulsen' in the garden is like a watercolor painting of a rose: a wash of artistically faded pink and green with few details. The rose in bloom is beautiful, though the blooms themselves, with only a minimum of fragrance, are not remarkable. Semi-double, light rose-pink on the inside of the petals with a slightly darker reverse, the flowers look as if they'd been tied on with bits of string all over the bush in such quantities that the string was no longer visible. 'Else Poulsen' is a background rose, a necessary setting to make the other roses shine. It's also a constant bloomer that performs like a professional in a hedge or border, or even as a specimen plant to add color to a particular space in the yard. In some areas this rose has a reputation for getting a little powdery mildew, but it is normally very tough and healthy. It has several sports that were supposed to be improvements on the original, but 'Else' has remained reliably in commerce and in gardens since the 1920's, while the "improved" varieties are lost and gone.

ERFURT
Hybrid Musk. Introduced 1939.

A sturdy rose and a sweet one, 'Erfurt' has large flowers for a Hybrid Musk. They are semi-double, wide, cupped, and ruffled, with a bright pink edge paling into a white center full of red-gold stamens. The strong musk fragrance is most noticeable when the flowers are fresh and the weather is warm. It's one of those perfumes to which people have varying responses: some perceive it as powerful, some as light and sweet, some not at all. I think it goes particularly well with strong-scented herbs like lavender and rosemary. The plant can be grown as a compact shrub with some pruning, but if left to grow naturally, 'Erfurt' has more of a spreading habit. It will easily reach 3 or 4 feet high by 5 or 6 feet wide, forming a mound of blossoms in spring and again in fall. There are some summer flowers, but they are scattered here and there rather than massed in a full display. The foliage is a semi-glossy dark green, with coppery new growth on dark canes—the contrast is beautiful with the pink flowers. As with other Hybrid Musks, this rose is very healthy and very tolerant of poor soils. It will tolerate a fair amount of shade—the flowers will actually keep their color and form better if they're protected from the full intensity of the sun.

EUTIN
Floribunda. Introduced 1940.

This rose has been collected so often from gardens across the South that it gathered quite a handful of study names before rosarians decided on the final identification. It has apparently been also sold by carefree nurserymen under the name of another rose, 'Seven Sisters', as well as a legitimate pseudonym of "Hoosier Glory." In Texas we prefer our own study name of "Rustler's Skyrocket," which is both easier to pronounce than the correct French name and more descriptive of the rose. The medium-sized flowers are true red, each blossom neat but not impressive; the effect is created by the huge clusters of up to 50 blooms. These masses of color are thrust out from a fairly open bush whose natural size is about 4 feet tall by 4 feet wide. Pruning can keep the bright green foliage thicker and the bush more shapely, but 'Eutin' is also capable of building up on itself to make a shrub that reaches to the gutters of a one-story house. It is neither the most beautiful plant nor the loveliest flower, and the fragrance is only moderate—though it improves when dried for potpourri. The

color impact is fantastic, however, and nobody looks at the details when the rose is blooming. 'Eutin' does its best to bloom all the time and in all circumstances. It is one of the most shade tolerant of all roses, and one of the most willing in difficult conditions.

FAIR BIANCA
Shrub. Introduced 1983.

If you were wishing for an Alba that would bloom repeatedly and fit in a small garden, David Austin has come up with a pretty good compromise in this rose. 'Fair Bianca' has classically beautiful flowers, deeply cupped and very double, that open from red-streaked buds into pure white with just a touch of creaminess in the depths. They are supposed to be myrrh-scented, but I'm not sure what myrrh smells like. To me they have an intense per-

fume of unmistakable licorice. The heaviest production of bloom is in the cooler weather of spring and fall, but there are a few flowers on the bush most of the time. The plant that supports these lovely flowers is small, rarely exceeding 3 feet in height in my garden, and not very impressive. The foliage is light green and only covers the plant really well in the first spring growth flush. It survives, however, in spite of non-English heat and being crowded by various perennials through the changing seasons—'Fair Bianca' is much tougher than it looks. This is a fine little rose for container culture, where it will be accessible for enjoying the perfume, or as part of a scented herb garden design.

THE FAIRY
Polyantha. Introduced 1932.

Everybody seems to know this rose, and nearly everybody seems to grow it. For a cascading bush to spill over a container or make a soft border in front of a large flower bed, 'The Fairy' is the first rose to come to mind—even after more than sixty years constantly in commerce. The flowers are small and double, produced in clusters all along the arching canes. They tend to be a strong pink in cool weather, lighter pink in the summer, and a faded white under intense direct sun. There's almost no scent at all, but the rose makes up for that by its performance in

the landscape. I've seen it used in almost every rose display garden, and a number of highway plantings besides. In most areas the thick covering of small, glossy leaves is bulletproof in terms of blackspot resistance, though 'The Fairy' can be defoliated occasionally by spider mites because the foliage is so low to the ground it's hard to reach with a hard water wash. 'The Fairy', at about 3 feet high and 4 feet wide, would contrast well with 'Pearl Drift' or make an interesting soft stairstep planting combined with little 'Sweet Chariot', either in the garden or in a grouping of containers. If you want to try the look of the same pretty pink clusters from a different angle, there's a Climbing Polyantha of the same name that is probably a sport of this rose.

FANTIN-LATOUR
Centifolia. Date of introduction unknown.

A found rose from an earlier century, 'Fantin-Latour' got rechristened and reintroduced during the last years of Queen Victoria's reign. The assumption is that it could be a much older rose, possibly a Centifolia-China cross rather than a pure Centifolia. Henri Fantin-Latour was a nineteenth-century painter whose flower studies were known for just the kind of lush romanticism that his namesake rose embodies in the garden. The very double flowers are blush pink swirls of delicately thin petals. Their rich fragrance is overpowering, and this rose blooms for at least a full month even in the zone 8 climate. 'Fantin-Latour' is a very big bush, mounding to 4 or 5 feet high and considerably wider—given time and the gardener's permission it can sprawl over quite a bit of territory. The canes, covered with a remarkable matte blue-green foliage that makes the flowers stand out spectacularly, are gradually arched over permanently under the weight of foliage and flowers. One rosarian friend ties ornamental bricks to the canes to train the recalcitrant wild ones into a more uniform cascading shape; her specimen plant is particularly lovely. This is one of the few old European roses that thrives in the South and needs no pampering, so perhaps it really does have China blood.

FELICIA
Hybrid Musk. Introduced 1928.

Hybrid Musk roses weren't exactly created for small gardens, but 'Felicia' is one of the most adaptable for this purpose. The semi-double, apricot-pink flowers, fading to pale peach under intense sun, are extremely sweet-scented. Their light clusters decorate a rather narrow bush that is easy to keep pruned to a 4- to 5-foot height. The smooth, rigid canes are not heavily branched; they tend to lean out from the base rather like those of a stiff climber. Cutting the rose back will keep it shrubbier and better covered by the light green foliage, but it can be allowed to develop to pillar-rose height. It will eventually reach as much as 9 or 10 feet this way, but it must be either trained when the canes are still young enough to be flexible, or simply fanned out flat on a trellis. The natural growth habit of the rose is not ideal for a specimen plant, but it works very well in a bed of large perennials, especially some of the big blue salvias that might smother a smaller or bushier rose, so that any lack of foliage is covered and the deliciously fragrant flowers are displayed to advantage. Like others of its class, 'Felicia' is a tough and healthy rose with a great deal of shade tolerance. It differs in being a fairly constant bloomer and a good cut flower.

FLOWER CARPET
Shrub. Introduced 1989.

Marketed as "The Environmental Rose," with a touted extra-long flowering season and minimal maintenance requirements, 'Flower Carpet' started out with a superb presentation and a lot to live up to. In just a few years of existence this German-bred variety has already earned six European awards and a reputation for cold hardiness and disease resistance. Rich pink with just a hint of coral in cool weather, the clusters of medium-sized double flowers open loosely to show a white eye and gold stamens. They have a strong Tea fragrance when just open and are very longlasting on the plant. On the down side, the spent petals cling unattractively, and in hot weather the flowers are sparse and bloom a very light, washed-out pink. 'Flower Carpet' is supposed to set hips, but I have yet to see any signs of fruit.

The plant, recommended for use as a groundcover or hanging basket specimen, reaches 2 or 3 feet high by 3 to 4 feet wide and has dark green, very shiny little leaves that cover the prickly canes thoroughly. The foliage is supposed to be disease resistant, requiring no spraying, but the plants I purchased on the first day of availability already had blackspot on them and continued to struggle with it until the weather cooled down. To 'Flower Carpet's' credit, only a small percentage of foliage is actually lost to the disease, but the shiny leaves make the black spots on bright yellow ground show up particularly well. On the whole, 'Flower Carpet' seems to be a reasonably healthy, fragrant rose with potential in the landscape, more unique in its marketing than in its character. As the accompanying literature suggests, it does better in cooler climates, but it's fairly shade tolerant, so try planting it in a location with some protection from direct afternoon sun if you want to grow it below upper zone 8. And look forward to the day when the majority of roses, old and new, will be grown and marketed as "environmental."

FORTUNE'S DOUBLE YELLOW
Miscellaneous Old Garden Rose. Introduced 1845.

Wang-jang-ve, or "yellow rose," was the Chinese name for this lovely climber when Robert Fortune collected it in a garden in Ningpo. It can't take cold weather at all, so only gardeners in zone 8 and below get to appreciate the flush of sweet-scented spring flowers. These flowers are large, loosely double cups of warm yellow flushed with rose and edged with crimson. They're carried individually on long prickly stems and make remarkably good cut flowers for indoor displays. The whole plant is fiercely prickly, which makes it painful to fuss with in the garden. It can be left alone to mound up into a wildlife-protecting 5- by 5-foot tangle of draping canes covered with pale green foliage, or, if you have the fortitude—and the gloves—to undertake the training, 'Fortune's Double Yellow' makes a spectacular climber. The delicate beauty of the flowers is traffic-stopping when spread out to the full length of the 12 to 15 foot canes. Extremely tolerant of any growing conditions as long as heat is included, this rose has naturalized in California, where it collected several pseudonyms over the years, including "San Raphael Rose."

green leaves accented by red new growth. 'Gruss an Aachen' is capable of getting both blackspot and powdery mildew, but it's a tough little rose in most situations and a constant producer of lovely flowers.

HANSA
Hybrid Rugosa. Introduced 1905.

If you like Rugosas, you'll be an immediate sucker for this variety. It has everything for which the class is admired, starting with large, silky, very double flowers of crimson-purple loaded with the delicious fragrance of roses mixed with cloves. The flowers are produced in small quantities very steadily throughout the growing season, with big flushes in both spring and fall. Spent blooms are replaced with an excellent crop of big, fat, shiny scarlet hips that have excellent flavor and culinary properties. The plant is large and sturdy, growing into an upright, vase-shaped bush almost as wide as it is tall—usually 4 or 5 feet in every direction. The leaves are tidy and very rugosed, looking not unlike deep green, semi-glossy cutouts of rhino hide. They turn dark burgundy and orange after a few fall frosts if the plant is growing in good sun. As with other Hybrid Rugosas, 'Hansa' will be grateful for a light, well-drained soil, mulch, and a little afternoon shade to cool off its roots and maintain good health in zones 8 and 9. These roses are invincible in the North; for us they can blackspot and lose foliage if allowed to get stressed by dense soil and heat.

HERITAGE
Shrub. Introduced 1984.

It would be easy to mistake the flowers of this rose for those of an old Centifolia. They are perfectly formed cups full of neatly arranged petals, always deliciously fragrant with a rich rose-and-honey scent. The color is pale pink, slightly darker in cool weather, and becomes a light peachy blush in the summer, when the flowers are smaller and have fewer petals so that the center of golden stamens is exposed. The bush that bears them is much more modern in habit. Straight, firm canes shoot up to 6 feet or more with minimal branching. New canes are produced often from the base, and they always bring fresh flowers with them. There are few prickles, though the ones that do exist are quite sharp and sturdy. The foliage is sparse during most of the growing season, with neatly pointed leaves of medium green mostly decorating the newest growth. 'Heritage' can blackspot and get pretty bald, but it's basically quite healthy and tough with no special cultivation requirements beyond good soil and basic care. Unless you want to grow this rose at the very back of the border, using its height to lift the flowers above tall perennials, you may prefer to prune it to about 4 feet. This will encourage even heavier blooming, plus making the flowers accessible so that their perfume can be properly enjoyed.

HERMOSA
China. Introduced before 1837.

No parentage is given for this wonderful rose, but it is assumed to be a Bourbon-China cross and has been moved in and out of each category over the years. It does-n't really matter where it belongs on paper, because it so obviously belongs in the garden. The double, blue-pink flowers are very globular when they cover the bush at their best in the spring and fall bloom seasons. The rest of the time they are still freely produced, but paler, smaller in size, and more open in nature. 'Hermosa' has a strong sweet fragrance whenever it blooms, suggestive of a mix-ture of the fruity China scent and the rosy Bourbon perfume. The plant is small, well-branched, and bushy, covered with neat blue-green foliage that makes an attractive foil for the blossoms. It tends toward a slightly ragged pattern of growth, mostly due to the habit of putting up long new flower-producing shoots and developing along them. Minimal shaping will keep 'Hermosa' more compact and make it an ideal rose for container gardening or for accenting a favorite garden feature. It's a tough, healthy bush that rarely has much trouble with insects or diseases.

ICEBERG
Floribunda. Introduced 1958.

An all-time favorite among white roses, 'Iceberg' is the standard by which other Floribundas are judged. The slightly scented flowers are medium-sized, double, loosely cupped, and ruffled, with a half-hidden center of golden stamens in the midst of petals whiter than pasteurized milk. They are constantly produced throughout the grow-ing season, though the summer blossoms are not as large and fine as those seen in cooler weather. Where there's no frost, 'Iceberg' will try to bloom straight through the win-ter, justifying its European name of 'Schneewittchen', or "snow witch." The shapely, healthy bush gets between 3 and 4 feet tall, staying fairly well covered with glossy, light green foliage except for occasional losses from a touch of blackspot. This rose is reasonably shade tolerant, and the flowers show up beauti-fully against a dark or shady background. 'Iceberg' has an excellent climbing sport, also a constant favorite among gardeners, that will reach more than 15 feet to cover a wall or even a small tree with the same pure white flowers.

IMPATIENT
Floribunda. Introduced 1982.

'Impatient' looks as if it should be a prima donna, but it performs in the gar-den like an old trooper. The vivid orange-red flowers, semi-double and neatly arranged around a center of very dark gold stamens, are almost shocking in intensi-ty—a color you might associate with a quick temper. They mix remarkably well, how-ever, with gray or silver herbs such as lamb's ears and artemisia; this rose can really brighten up an overly quiet herb garden. There is only a little bit of fragrance, easi-

LA BELLE SULTANE
Gallica. Introduced circa 1795.

Not all old European roses have a hard time in the South. This rose in particular will thrive, even in blasting heat and poor soil—in fact, not only will it thrive, but it will sucker so enthusiastically you'll soon have a thicket where you once had a single plant. This rose is an argument for grafting, but it needs a rootstock to confine its vigor, not to make it stronger. Suckering aside, 'La Belle Sultane' is a wonderful rose. The fragrant, deep crimson, nearly single flowers fade to that gorgeous Gallica gray-purple—considered a fault when it was introduced, but a definite plus to our modern tastes. Once the long (six to eight weeks) spring bloom is over, the plant quits flowering and begins to set some hips, under the impression that dormancy will quickly follow. When you're two hundred years old, it seems you don't easily learn new tricks. Summer is always a shock, causing some leaf drop—and more suckering. In fall there will be a whole new set of foliage, which turns wine red and dark orange after a few frosts. The slender, whiplike, 3- to 4-foot canes, waving about freely once released from the weighty burden of leaves and flowers, also turn dark red in a sunny autumn garden. 'La Belle Sultane' is as handsome in the winter garden as a clump of red dogwood, making a colorful contrast with bright yellow daffodils, but I've learned to grow it—with the winter bulbs—in a large container. Digging up the suckers is time consuming, and I've run out of friends who don't already have a start of this ancient but enthusiastic rose.

LA FRANCE
Hybrid Tea. Introduced 1867.

One of the very first Hybrid Teas, 'La France' was the start of a revolution in rose breeding. Though considered the prototype of a class formed by crossing Teas and Hybrid Perpetuals, you can't really tell from this sweet, old-fashioned-looking cultivar that it is the dividing line between Old Garden Roses and all modern varieties. The fragrant blossoms are large and double, their pointed buds opening to show petals of silver pink with a warm pink reverse—the effect is of light and shadow in play across the flower. They are carried on a bush that grows much like other Tea roses, which were also hybrids within their own class: full-foliaged and broad, about 4 feet tall and nearly as wide. The breeder himself, Guillot (fils), thought this rose was possibly the seedling of a Tea he had introduced earlier, 'Madame Falcot'. Others felt the bloodlines were a Tea ('Madame Bravy') crossed with a Hybrid Perpetual ('Madame Victor Verdier'). There's a lot that could be said here about keeping careful records, but Mon. Guillot couldn't have known how important the rose was going to be, especially to generations of future exhibitors struggling with precise classification on their rose labels. In the garden, 'La France' is simply a lovely and healthy rose that produces fragrant flowers generously throughout the growing season.

LA MARNE
Polyantha. Introduced 1915.

There are some roses that were born for the landscape, destined, as it were, for low-maintenance greatness. 'La Marne' is one of these. Its medium-sized pink and white flowers, cupped and ruffled, are produced in relaxed clusters all over the surface of a 5-foot-high by 3-foot-wide bush covered with dark green, shiny foliage. It stays almost constantly in bloom and grows very well in unimproved soil; beautiful specimens are often seen in old cemeteries. There's a slight salmon tinge to the pink flowers that makes 'La Marne' hard to blend with the blue-pink blossoms of many older rose varieties in the garden, but by itself or with compatible colors this rose is outstanding. The only possible drawback to landscape use, as a specimen, hedge, or mass planting, is that the blossoms bleach nearly to white in the intense summer sun. The richness of flowers and foliage in cool weather, however, has to be seen to be believed. 'La Marne' is extremely disease resistant, though I have seen powdery mildew on it when planted in deep shade. There's almost no scent, but there are also very few prickles, so it's a good choice for high traffic areas that need some brightening up.

LADY BANKS' ROSE, *Rosa banksiae*
Species. Cultivated from 1796.

There are four known clones of the Species, *Rosa banksiae*, all spring-blooming and all beautiful. The single white, felt to be the original wild form, is *R. b. normalis.* The single yellow is *R. b. lutescens.* Then come two more familiar forms: *R. b. lutea*—the beloved double yellow— and *R. banksiae banksiae*—the double white with the double name, whose violet-scented clusters of tiny pompoms were the first to be widely known to gardeners. This last type, growing to 20 feet or more with thornless canes and narrow, graceful, three-leaflet leaves, was the one first named for the wife of botanist and explorer (what a great job) Sir Joseph Banks. It was introduced to the West in 1807; the wild form actually had been collected earliest but was left struggling miserably in a cold and isolated Scottish garden until 1877. This species has a much longer history in its native China: *Rosa banksiae* is one of four types of roses mentioned in Li Shi-Chen's sixteenth-century medical book as being used for medicinal purposes.

Between the double yellow and the double white Lady Banks' Rose there isn't much to choose. Both are magnificently vigorous and completely thornless, with foliage that will stay evergreen in zones 9 and 10. The yellow is more colorful, while the white has an advantage in fragrance and the status of "largest rose in the world." There's a white Lady Banks' in Tombstone, Arizona that covers more than 8,000 square feet of arbor—the prunings are carried away in pick-up loads. Ideally, you'd want to plant this rose, white or yellow, where you wouldn't have to prune it but could just let it go as it pleased. This is an excellent rose for naturalizing, growing into trees, or using to smother an ugly shed. It's reputed to be deer proof and tolerant of sandy soils as well as clay, and it is limited only by intolerance for cold temperatures—pests and diseases leave it alone.

LAMARQUE
Noisette. Introduced 1830.

Given a mild climate, there is no rose more beautiful than 'Lamarque' in the winter. The clusters of medium-sized, double, lemon-white flowers are seriously fragrant, and unlike some roses they don't have to be warm to smell good. Bringing them into the house, however, does heat up the oils in the petals so that even more perfume is released. Only a series of hard frosts will cause dormancy in this rose that thrives in cool, but not cold, weather. 'Lamarque' also blooms heavily in the spring, with some smaller flowers produced at sporadic intervals through the heat of the summer.

The foliage is soft green, gracefully pointed and lush, with only a little blackspot now and then to bother it. This is a big climber, not just because the canes can reach to 20 feet, but because it builds up over a few years into a massive plant unless you choose to thin out some of the oldest canes each year. New canes are quite flexible and easy to work with in training, so if you plan to use it on a trellis or against the house instead of cascading loosely over a wall or arbor, it's a good idea to keep up with this kind of grooming. Either way, make sure your supports are adequate for the weight of this lovely rose.

LAVENDER LASSIE
Hybrid Musk. Introduced 1960.

Sometimes there's a place that just cries out to be decorated by a climbing rose, but simply doesn't get enough bright sun—the north wall of the house, for example, under the overhang of the eaves. Fortunately, there's at least one climber that will perform in a situation like this. 'Lavender Lassie' is remarkably tolerant of bright shade, steadily producing clusters of medium-sized, lightly fragrant, blue-pink pompoms with a minimum of direct sun. The canes reach 12 to 15 feet and are well-covered by disease-resistant, medium-green foliage even with poor light. In the sun, this rose will bloom in great profusion, especially during the spring and fall peak seasons. 'Lavender Lassie' can be pruned into a fat, leafy bush about 5 feet in every direction, but it's so good as a climber that it's a shame to waste the talent. The one exception is that you might want to include it in an informal rose hedge, especially if using similarly versatile Hybrid Musks such as 'Belinda' and 'Prosperity'.

LE VÉSUVE
China. Introduced 1825.

Some suggestion that this may really be a Bourbon hybrid or even an early Tea rose, but it fits well enough where it is in terms of garden performance. The good-sized, very double flowers are a pretty muddle of petals in shades of light and warm pink, with dark carmine petals at the very back. They are carried in nodding clusters amidst a wealth of shapely, pointed leaves on a compact bush that usually gets 3 or 4 feet high and nearly as wide. The fragrance is variable—sometimes sweetly fruit, other times non-existent—depending upon the weather and the age of the blossom. This rose is an excellent choice for both the landscape, where it will remain colorful and healthy throughout the blooming season, and the container garden. 'Le Vésuve' can live a long time in half of a whiskey barrel, with pale pink portulaca filling in underneath and spilling over the sides. It's particularly elegant in the herb garden, where soft mounds of scented silver make the pink flowers glow. In high humidity this rose may get some blackspot, but in most gardens it will remain resistant to both disease and insects.

LICHTERLOH
Floribunda. Introduced 1955.
Produced by a cross between a medium-sized Floribunda ('Red Favorite') and the vigorous climber 'New Dawn', this rose flew in the face of obvious genetics and turned out smaller than either parent. Even the flowers are small, barely bigger than those of a large Mini, but the semi-double bright scarlet blossoms are carried in good-sized clusters and repeat well through the growing season. With the background of shiny foliage, this rose could hold its own in a red-and-green contest against any poinsettia, but by Christmas the flowers have been replaced by sprays of large, round, bright orange hips. Both flowers and hips are stiffly thrust out from the bush, as if 'Lichterloh' were doing its best to stretch to larger dimensions. Over time the plant can build up to 3 feet in height, but it usually stays rather open in form, with the foliage only giving really good coverage when it first comes out in the spring. 'Lichterloh' is a nice rose to use in a situation where you plan to grow things through it—ornamental alliums, for example. It's particularly nice in a container with some Society garlic for a summer accent and early daffodils for winter color. It's a healthy rose on the whole and a useful one where reliable color is wanted—not bushy, but definitely bright.

LINDA CAMPBELL
Hybrid Rugosa. Introduced 1990.
This rose was named by breeder Ralph Moore in honor of the wife of Dr. William Campbell. 'Linda Campbell' is distinctive among Hybrid Rugosas for the bright clear red of its flowers. They are produced nearly constantly throughout the growing season in big eye-catching clusters of five to twenty-five medium-sized blossoms, cupped and loosely double. There's no fragrance, which is unusual for a member of this class, but the possibilities for this variety in the landscape are exciting. You'd

never know this rose had a Miniature as one parent, since the dense bush gets easily 6-feet high by 8 wide. Hidden behind a wealth of rough, dark green, semi-glossy leaves, fortunately the canes have few thorns, so if you want to try and keep it clipped within slightly smaller boundaries you should be able to do so without serious injury. 'Linda Campbell' is cold hardy, but also more tolerant than many rugosas of heat and tight soil. This rose has become a favorite with Grounds Director Leonard Veazey of The American Rose Center in Shreveport, Louisiana, because it performs so well in the landscape and is so disease resistant.

LINDEE
Found Polyantha. No date of introduction known.

The fat clusters of tiny white flowers suggest that this small foundling—shared with the Antique Rose Emporium by Mike Lindee, of Houston, who got it from his grandmother—is a Polyantha. On the other hand, it's very similar in growth and flowering habits to the Miniature variety 'Blue Mist', so it may just as easily be a lost Mini. Either way "Lindee" is a handsome little rose, filling out to 2 or 3 feet in every direction, and very useful in the garden. The flowers are produced in successive flushes, with scattered blossoms in between the peaks of bloom. They are double and snow white, opening flat from tiny buds to show a charming little tuft of golden stamens. Spent blossoms tend to cling while the fresh ones are opening, but a brisk wind or a good shake by the hand of the gardener will knock away most of the tired petals and save tedious grooming with pruners. The neat, pointed leaves on this rose are as tiny as the flowers and as thickly produced. They get a little blackspot seasonally, but any foliage losses are quickly made up with new growth. Much bushier than most little roses, "Lindee" can be clipped into a neat ball until new sprays of flowers push up to upset the shape. It's an ideal plant for a semi-formal low hedge, or a container garden, or to hide any bare canes under a taller rose.

LITTLE BUCKAROO
Miniature. Introduced 1956.

This is a small rose on a serious bush; in spite of descriptions that list it as 14 to 16 inches, I've seen it grown as a thick hedge nearly 5 feet high. The flowers are tiny, double, crimson-and-white stars, very much the same color as the old red China roses. 'Little Buckaroo' was actually collected as an unknown at one point and grouped with the found Chinas until its identity was established. One of the things that helped sort it out was the light fragrance of green apples, a characteristic of varieties—including this one—that have been bred from *Rosa wichuraiana*. It has narrow, neatly pointed, glossy leaflets that combine to form bronze-green foliage thickly covering the twiggy and well-branched plant. 'Little Buckaroo' is extremely healthy and very tolerant of an assortment of growing conditions. It's obviously much too large a plant to treat as a true Miniature, but it's a reliably steady bloomer that performs remarkably well in the landscape with very little care.

LOUIS PHILIPPE
China. Introduced 1834.

In Texas we're proud of this rose because we're pretty sure how it got here: almost certainly it was brought home by Lorenzo deZavala following his stint as Texian Ambassador to France. We do not know, however, exactly which of a multitude of red China roses is really 'Louis Philippe'. It's particularly well confused with 'Cramoisi Supérieur', a similar variety introduced only two years earlier. Both of these are described in period catalogs as having cupped, double flowers of rich, brilliant crimson, with the difference that 'Cramoisi' is supposed to have occasional white streaks on the petals and 'Louis' is supposed to have a paler center. Since these two characteristics have both been seen in almost every candidate for either name, varying with the season and the soil, most rosarians have a tendency to scream and run when asked for positive identification.

The rose that gardeners are now used to as 'Louis Philippe' seems to have the paler center most of the time, cupped around a delicious fruity fragrance. The 4-foot-high, constantly-blooming bush is extremely hardy in heat and poor soils—either sandy or clay. 'Louis Philippe' was described as naturalized in Florida long ago, so they may well have the best candidate. The same rose that grows there—or a very similar one—is found in yards and cemeteries across the South. I've even seen it in one public garden in Charleston, South Carolina, blooming heavily with half its roots exposed after hurricane Hugo had knocked it over. No matter which cupped, fragrant red China rose you personally grow, it's bound to be one of the best in your garden. Should you want to really fill your garden with this particular kind of beauty, there's a very good climbing rose still available that is supposed to be a sport of 'Cramoisi Supérieur'.

MADAME ALFRED CARRIÈRE
Noisette. Introduced 1879.

Named for the wife of a French scientist who had an interest in rose breeding, 'Madame Alfred Carrière' is the Noisette most likely to be still blooming in January. It's hardier than many other cultivars in this class—perhaps containing some Bourbon genes—and cool weather turns the pale flowers pink. They are usually nearly white, with just a hint of blush, and produced in large, loose cups with an intense perfume. The canes of this rose are long, smooth (but not thornless) and very stiff. It will reach 20 feet as a climber, but some gardeners choose to cut it back and grow it as a tall bush in the 6- to 8-foot range. It's a good idea to start early if you plan to do any tricky training, because the canes aren't very flexible once they mature. 'Madame Alfred' is known for willingness to grow on north walls in England, but it will probably do better if it gets plenty of sunshine. It's likely to get some blackspot and powdery mildew from time to time, but it's never seriously affected either in vigor or in frequency of bloom.

MADAME GRÉGOIRE STAECHELIN
Large-flowered Climber. Introduced 1927.

Created by Spanish breeder Pedro Dot from a cross between white 'Frau Karl Druschki' and an early red Hybrid Tea, 'Chateau de Clos Vougeot', this unpronounceable child of unpronounceable parents is often known simply as "Spanish Beauty." It's one of the best modern climbers available, bearing several flushes of large, very fragrant soft pink blossoms with a darker pink reverse. The flowers are double, but open, showing a broad center of dark gold stamens surrounded by ruffled petals. This rose blooms very early in the season, and if not dead-headed will produce an excellent crop of large, pear-shaped orange-red hips by autumn. The foliage, known for good disease resistance, is a dark, semi-glossy olive green that complements the flowers beautifully. The canes can reach up to 15 feet and this rose is both shade tolerant and accepting of poor soils, so it's a good choice for training into an open-branched deciduous tree. 'Madame Grégoire Staechelin' won several awards when first introduced and remains extremely popular in Europe, but it's not nearly as well known in the States—a situation which should be corrected.

MADAME HARDY
Damask. Introduced 1832.

Named for the breeder's wife—almost always the sign of something especially good—'Madame Hardy' remains one of the most popular of Old Garden Roses. This is partly because of the memorable flowers: large, very white, very fragrant and very double, the petals at the center tucked in and buttoned down with a green eye so that no stamens are visible. It's also partly because this rose tolerates such a wide range of growing conditions. The lush, soft, gray-green foliage is tougher than it looks, resisting both pests and diseases better than many modern varieties. The canes are flexible but vigorous, reaching as much as 10 feet in length, so 'Madame Hardy' can be trained very successfully as a pillar rose. It can also be left to form a relaxed shrub roughly 5 feet high and equally wide, or guided into sprawling over a fence—stone or wrought iron for aesthetic choice. As with many of the old European varieties, 'Madame Hardy' only blooms once a year. This gives you time to prepare for the best possible show by cosseting it with good soil, regular water, and mulch, protecting its roots from the heat while you plan next spring's garden party to show off its perfumed beauty.

MADAME ISAAC PEREIRE
Bourbon. Introduced 1881.

There are probably more roses with names beginning "Madame" than any other prefix except *Rosa*—fourteen pages of them are recorded in *Modern Roses 10*. European hybridizers were obviously a courtly group and knew who held the power in the land. This particular Madame Pereire was a banker's wife, and the rose christened in her honor is, most appropriately, an asset to the garden. The shapely flowers are very large and extremely double, often quartered, with outer petals that reflex back so it looks as if the blossoms are straining to bare their beauties to the world. At the risk of sounding over-enthusiastic, I have to say that both their color and their fragrance are gorgeous—the one a rich purple-tinged rose and the other a deep, soul-satisfying blend of intense perfumes. I would grow this rose even if the flowers came on a plastic bush from Wal-Mart, so the slight awkwardness of the real plant is easy to overlook. The new canes are long, 5 or 6 feet as a rule, so that even if you prune 'Madame Isaac' as a nice fat bush you'll still have to deal with this wildness. This is perhaps the best rose available for pegging, and it will also work well as a short pillar if you decide to keep the natural form. The foliage is large and deep green, proof against just about everything except blackspot. Any leaves lost to this disease over the summer will be fully replaced by the fall bloom season so the best flowers of the year will have a good background; 'Madame Isaac' doesn't bloom constantly, but when it does, it's real nice.

MADAME LOUIS LÉVÊQUE
Moss. Introduced 1898.

Moss roses aren't the easiest class to grow in the South; they tend to struggle with the heat anywhere below zone 8, and some have trouble below zone 7. If you like the unique scent produced by the glandular hairs on the buds (Victorian ladies felt it was an aphrodisiac) and want to try a few varieties, look for cultivars like 'Madame Louis Lévêque' that have the repeat-blooming 'Autumn Damask' in their background. Not only are they more likely to survive the warm weather and lack of dormancy, but they will often have at least a small second flush of bloom in the fall. This particular variety, named in honor of the breeder's wife, has been one of the most reliable in my experience. It stays smaller than it would in the North, reaching just over 3 feet. In the spring small clusters of fragrant mossy buds open to very large, double, dark pink blossoms with their own, completely different, perfume. The canes are slender and flexible, with a dusting of small, narrow prickles. The foliage is a dark olive green, mostly produced in bunches just behind the flowers. In summer the slender plant may be as naked as a plucked chicken, though from heat stress rather than disease. The leaves return in the autumn, and sometimes there are a few more of the beautiful flower clusters if the root zone has been kept as cool as possible with regular watering and thick mulch.

MADAME PLANTIER
Hybrid Alba. Introduced 1835.

Thought to be a cross between an Alba and either a Noisette or *Rosa moschata*, this rose has enough oriental blood to thrive in the South at least to the bottom of zone 8. 'Madame Plantier', like 'Madame Hardy', was named for the wife of the proud breeder, and its pure white, double flowers are rather similar to those of that cultivar, except that they are a little smaller and rarely show the green pip in the center. They are fragrant and quite lovely, but they aren't the primary reason for growing this rose. It's the canes—sleek, slightly wavy, silver-gray, and nearly  thornless, cascading in a broad arch from the base of the plant—that make this an important feature of any garden it graces. You can't grow this rose in a small space,

buds to white blossoms with just a hint of blush. They are double, but flat, so that the golden center of stamens is exposed, and lastingly fragrant with a sweet scent that carries in the air. The leaves are also large for a Polyantha, making up a thick foliage of rich green that covers the 4-foot-high by 3-foot-wide plant from top to bottom. Rarely does this rose show any signs of disease or pest trouble, and when it does it's so mild and fleeting that you can happily ignore it. There are a few small, tender prickles under the midribs of the leaves, but otherwise 'Marie Pavié' can be handled without pain. It's a great rose for high traffic areas, or container gardens, or by the kitchen door where you want the scent to drift in while you do dishes. The dense foliage also makes it a fine choice for a protective low hedge on the north side of the vegetable garden: even in winter dormancy the plant is so well branched that it will break the force of a cold wind sweeping down on your broccoli.

MARTHA GONZALES
Found China. No date of introduction known.

One of the scary things about collecting unknown varieties of old roses is that they may have grown in a certain place for generations and be as hardy as old boot leather, but they can still vanish from the world almost overnight. This particular little red China rose was spotted in a garden in Navasota, Texas, by two rustling rosarians (Pam Puryear and Joe Woodard) who saw it from a block away. The scentless flowers are rather small and only semi-double, but their rich, glowing scarlet shows up vividly against neatly pointed foliage of dark green. Each flower has a bit of white at the center, behind the gold stamens, and often a streak of white in at least one petal. The whole bush is dense and compact, remarkably disease resistant, and covered with successive flushes of bright flowers throughout the growing season. It makes an excellent low hedge, container rose, or even a good subject for bedding-out in the landscape. None of the other China roses fill exactly the same niche, so it would be a real shame to have missed this little treasure. It was study-named for the gardener in whose yard it was collected—she had a number of plants of this variety growing mixed with 'Old Blush' and 'Mrs. Dudley Cross'—and re-introduced to commerce through the Antique Rose Emporium. Just a few years later Señora Gonzales passed away, and now her rose garden is gone.

MARY MANNERS
Hybrid Rugosa. Introduced 1970.

There are only two rugosa cultivars that actually do better in the South than in the North. 'Mary Manners' is one of them, and it is assumed to be a sport of the other, 'Sarah Van Fleet'. The bloodlines of these roses are uncertain, but the garden performance is a sure thing. The large, double, snow white flowers are produced consistently from spring to fall, though the summer flowers are somewhat smaller and have fewer petals. The fragrance is unusually sweet for a member of this class, not as potent or as spicy as you might expect, but still quite nice when the flowers are

just opening. Neither this nor its sport mother set any hips. The bush is very large and dense, rapidly reaching 5 or 6 feet in height and nearly the same in width, with a quite remarkable number of sharp prickles on the new growth. The rough, semi-glossy foliage is bright green and disease resistant, though it can get some rust during the summer. 'Mary Manners' is an outstanding landscape specimen, reasonably tolerant of poor or tight soils and a good candidate for a hedge or screen between different areas of the garden. It's particularly nice against a dark wall where the clean green and white shows up to best advantage.

MARY ROSE
Shrub. Introduced 1983.

This is one of the most reliable David Austin cultivars for both cool and warm climate gardening, as well as a favorite of American Rose Society exhibitors. It carries one of the highest ARS ratings for shrub roses, and the name of a famous flagship of King Henry VIII. The flowers are very double, starting out as beautiful, precisely arranged cups of petals and gradually relaxing their need for control as they open into mature blossoms. The final result is a sweet, rather blowzy muddle of rich pink petals with a nice Damask fragrance. 'Mary Rose' is a good repeat-bloomer, though in hot weather the flowers have fewer petals and are a much lighter shade of pink. The plant is a handsome, well-branched, upright bush to about 4 feet with rather small foliage of a rich green color. It can get blackspot or mildew, but it's rarely severely affected. I've seen this rose growing fairly successfully in the dry hills of the California wine country, in the Bishop's Herb Garden at the National Cathedral in Washington, DC, and in humid New Orleans.

MAURINE NEUBERGER
Miniature. Introduced 1989.

A Miniature rose bush in full bloom always looks to me like a bouquet of rosebuds. In this case the association is particularly appropriate, for red rosebuds stand for "pure and lovely" in the Victorian language of flowers, and 'Maurine Neuberger' is the purest of reds with a very lovely form. The lightly scented flowers are completely double and they unfurl in classic Hybrid Tea form, though reduced in scale as if you were looking at a big rose through the wrong end of the telescope. At maturity the petals roll into points, so that the fully open flowers look like layered stars. 'Maurine' is a reliable bloomer, though not quite as pretty during the summer as during the cooler weather of fall and spring. The plant is tidy and compact, growing to just over 2 feet. It keeps the matte green foliage fairly well throughout the growing season, though it can be affected somewhat by mildew in dry climates. This rose makes a fine color accent in the garden, especially when grouped cupped maturity. They are extremely fragrant and make excellent exhibition subjects, or great cut flowers for indoors. The stems are long and very strong, so this rose will also serve for a long-stemmed bouquet to present on a romantic occasion. The bush is tall and narrow, reaching 4 feet in most conditions and shooting up to 6 feet with extra fertilizer or a little shade. The canes are very dark, and the combination of these with the red roses and the large, forest green leathery leaves makes a strikingly sophisticated statement in the garden. I like to bunch several plants together when a fuller bush is desirable, but sometimes the simple elegance of 'Mister Lincoln' by itself is all that's wanted. This variety is supposed to get some mildew when conditions are right, but not even the great can be always free from adversity.

MRS. B.R. CANT
Tea. Introduced 1901.

British rose breeder Benjamin R. Cant waited until he'd been in business almost fifty years before he introduced this rose and named it for his wife. Having found a plant that would assure her posterity forever among discerning gardeners, he died shortly afterwards. Cants of Colchester, however—started over a hundred years before B.R's time—is still in business and still creating good roses. None of them are like 'Mrs. B. R.', but it has always stood apart from the crowd. Part of the reason for this is the size of the bush—it's not hard to be noticed when you tower over your classmates. 'Mrs. B. R. Cant' will easily reach 6 feet in every direction, and it's even more comfortable when the dimensions increase to 8 by 8 feet. The flowers, too, are distinctive: large and cabbagey even in the summer, huge and quartered when cool weather increases the petal count. They have a good Tea scent and a shimmering rose color that darkens to crimson when exposed to intense sunlight. This giantess among Tea roses can afford to make concessions to us little people, so it is willing to grow in almost any condition—in or out of the garden. It's a common graveyard find for rose collectors throughout the South, where it will often be the biggest flowering shrub in sight.

MRS. DUDLEY CROSS
Tea. Introduced 1907.

Along with "Maggie" and one or another of the red Chinas, this is probably the most frequently encountered Old Garden Rose in Texas. There are several reasons for that. It blooms constantly, with large, Tea-scented double flowers of creamy yellow edged with pink. It roots very easily from cuttings, making it a natural to share with neighbors and gardening friends. It's moderate in size for a Tea rose, forming a v-shaped leafy bush about 3 or 4 feet high and nearly as wide that will fit into most front yards. All those good points would keep it moving from hand to hand and garden to garden, but, best of all, 'Mrs. Dudley Cross' is also thornless. There's a very similar-looking variety named 'Marie van Houtte' with which this rose is often confused, but 'Marie' is not only a much larger plant but quite well armed.

Unless you have a very big garden to fill up, 'Mrs. Dudley Cross' is by far the most useful of the two plants. Because of its disease resistance, compact size, and tolerance for poor soils this rose can be easily managed as a hedge, but it also looks nice in any garden bed or as a specimen plant in a place of special honor—ask any of the hundreds of little old ladies who grow it that way.

MRS. OAKLEY FISHER
Hybrid Tea. Introduced 1921.

This is about the most unlikely Hybrid Tea I've ever seen. Each five-petaled copper yellow flower, with a center of dark orange stamens, is only a few inches wide, and they're produced in small clusters on a fat, twiggy bush that barely reaches 3 feet high. It's a fantastic garden plant, because it stays healthy, blooms constantly and the bright, dainty flowers stand out to perfection against the small, dark olive green foliage. The bush is very well branched and stays fairly compact between prunings. It would make a great Floribunda or small Shrub, but, after all, what's in a name? A rose is a rose . . . and this one is not only pretty but smells really, really sweet, even the just-opening buds. I've used 'Mrs. Oakley Fisher', alternating with the crimson Floribunda 'Valentine', to line a long path leading to the door of a country Bed and Breakfast. I've also planted it, in the ornamental gardens of The Organic Plant Institute, in beds where it will draw the eye to other single-flowered plants in complementary shades. It's a beautiful mixer, blending with all sorts of roses—old or new—and most perennials.

MUSK ROSE, *Rosa moschata*
Species. Cultivated by 1540.

This fine, historic rose, the subject of many a piece of poetry over the centuries, and parent of many important varieties, was almost lost forever because it isn't cold-hardy. A related species, *R. moschata nepalensis*, was introduced in the late 1800's, and since the newcomer was hardier and more vigorous, the true Musk Rose began to fade from sight. The differences between the two were obvious to concerned rosarians: the impostor grows into a massive climber more than 20 feet long and blooms in the early spring, while the Musk Rose forms a thick shrub only 6 or 7 feet tall on the average and has an unusual bloom season that doesn't start until early summer. Fortunately, the true variety was rediscovered, both in England and in the United States, by rosarians who knew what to look for, and it's now back in commerce instead of hidden away in graveyards and ancient gardens. The flowers of the Musk Rose aren't particularly beautiful. They tend to be insignificant when single and messy little clumps of petals when double; this rose sports freely back and forth with both types. When it's in full bloom, however, the clusters of snowy white scent the air for 15 feet in every direction. The bush is attractive even when there are no flowers, with a good covering of shapely, pointed leaves of rich green. Other than a little blackspot, this rose is very successful in the warm climate of the South.

open, rather arching style. The semi-glossy leaves are deep green and very healthy, even in partial shade, and the canes are smooth, with only a few prickles. The bush can get 4 feet high and 5 feet wide if grown *au natural*, or pruned into a more modestly sized hedge, or persuaded into making a 6- or 7-foot pillar rose. It's one of the few roses that I would never want to be without, not just for reasons of health and beauty but because of the incredible perfume.

OKLAHOMA
Hybrid Tea. Introduced 1964.

I know of at least one local nursery who sells this variety with a second tag attached that says "The Black Rose," because that's how their customers describe it to each other, so they ask for it that way. The flowers are amazingly dark red, with ebony velvet shadows in the depths of the high-centered blooms. They are double, very classic in form, and very, very fragrant. The large leaves are dark green and leathery, with little gloss, so the whole plant seems to support the common nickname. It's very healthy for a Hybrid Tea, if you can get a virus-free start; you may want to order through the mail rather than purchasing it at a local retail nursery. 'Oklahoma' is worth some trouble—it grows well as a handsome, leafy bush to 3 or 4 feet tall, blends just fine with most other shades of roses and keeps up a steady production of damask-scented flowers for the garden or indoors. It would make an interesting vertical accent next to the arching form of 'Nur Mahal' in a garden devoted to fragrance. There's a climbing sport available, very nice if you can grow it against a light background that will show up the flowers and let them be appreciated.

OLD BLUSH
China. Introduced 1752.

First of the everblooming Chinese roses to be introduced to Europe, and one of the most prolific rose parents of all time, 'Old Blush' is a longtime friend of gardeners because of its reliably recurrent bloom. It will keep going year 'round if there's no frost, following each wave of semi-double, dark-veined bluish pink flowers with a crop of round, yellow-orange hips that are very sweet to the taste. The lightly scented flowers aren't especially beautiful, being often irregular in form and inclined to wash out in the sun, but their sheer profusion led to several common nicknames, including "Common Monthly" and "Old Pink Daily." Under the latter name this familiar variety was given its very own assigned meaning in the Victorian language of flowers: "Thy smile I aspire to," while most of the others were simply lumped together by color designation.

The bush is a handsome landscape plant, reaching 5 or 6 feet high and nearly as wide in just a few years' time. It's well covered with nicely pointed foliage of medium green that is rarely affected by insects or disease. It makes an excellent specimen to accent an area in need of constant color, and it's so tolerant of poor soils and extreme heat that it's one of the best rose choices for hedging, windbreaks, or barrier planting. 'Old Blush' even has history to confirm this, because it was used on Réunion Island (formerly the Isle de Bourbon) as an agricultural hedge rose, along with the Autumn Damask. From their chance union sprang the entire class of Bourbon roses.

ORANGES 'N' LEMONS
Shrub. Introduced 1992.

Old is good, but new can be equally wonderful. 'Oranges 'n' Lemons' is proof that breeders really do think of gardeners, not just exhibitors and the cut flower industry, when selecting varieties for introduction. The medium-sized flowers on this rose are as vivid as any Floribunda: striped bright orange and yellow, with orange streaks and spatters on the yellow portions of the petals. The form is double, but open, so that the stamens can be seen at the center of a mature blossom. There's nothing even remotely shy or bashful on the whole plant. Fragrance is excellent, and best of all is the big healthy bush that supports the floral display. 'Oranges 'n' Lemons' will reach between 4 and 6 feet tall either grafted or on its own roots, and it spreads nearly as wide as it is high with a good covering of its electric flowers on all sides. The foliage is a glossy dark green and seems fairly disease resistant well into zone 8. This rose hasn't been available long enough to fully prove itself, but it looks very good so far.

PÂQUERETTE
Polyantha. Introduced 1875.

I'm sorry, but I can't help myself: I think this rose is really cute. The tiny, double flowers are so neatly grouped and so sweetly rounded, with their fragrant little cups of purest white; and the small plant is so tidily covered with the little green leaves—it's like a child on best behavior, pretending to be an adult. 'Pâquerette's' garden performance, however, is perfectly sound. This is supposed to be the first of the Polyantha class, assuming that we have the correct rose in commerce, and it is listed as a dwarf seedling of some double-flowered Multiflora, with China or Tea influence suspected. The result is a small but tough rose that blooms constantly in large clusters, tolerates poor soil and heat, and is highly resistant to most rose problems. It's a perfect plant for a small container, for edging a bed or any use for which a Miniature rose might be chosen. It doesn't make a big splash, visually, in a mixed bed, but it looks charming poking through the foliage of other, larger flowers—a small picture to enjoy within in the garden as a whole.

PAUL NEYRON
Hybrid Perpetual. Introduced 1869.

When elderly Southern ladies tell you that their mothers grew "cabbage roses," it often turns out that they mean 'Paul Neyron'. It's not truly a Cabbage Rose, because that's the common name for the Centifolia class, but it is one of only a few roses whose flowers are nearly as big as an actual, vegetable, cabbage. On a good fall day 'Paul Neyron' can produce richly fragrant, cerise pink blossoms packed with petals and as much as seven inches wide, overwhelming the heart of any gardener with a secret yearning for "bigger" and "more." True, these immense blossoms are produced infrequently on a measly sort of bush, usually just a handful of slender, nearly

PERLE D'OR
Polyantha. Introduced 1884.

In spite of the nickname "Yellow Cécile Brunner," this is a very distinctive rose that is hard to confuse with any other once you get to know it. The buds are the rich orange of a freshly cut ripe apricot, and they are long and beautifully formed—perfect for a lapel vase. They open to attractive pompom-type flowers of golden pink, with the silky outer petals all neatly curled back and the inner petals tucked into a center knot. The light, sweet scent of the blossoms is lost as they age, and the flowers bleach almost white in the summer sun, but 'Perle d'Or' will replace spent flowers quickly with new flushes of bloom. The plant grows just under 4 feet in most gardens—smaller in the North, and much larger in zones 9 or 10. Its habit is erect and well-branched, with the flowers produced mostly in clusters that are thrust up a little above the bush. The foliage is light green, thick, and fairly healthy, ignoring occasional leaves lost to blackspot. 'Perle d'Or' tolerates any conditions but will bloom most heavily in good, rich soil and look most beautiful against a dark background with the flower color protected by a little afternoon shade.

PIERRINE
Miniature. Introduced 1988.

This is one of those crossover roses: like a song that makes both the country and the pop charts, 'Pierrine' is a good performer both on the exhibition bench and in the garden. The flowers are coral pink, double, and perfectly formed in the classic high-centered Hybrid Tea style, with a mild Damask-Tea fragrance. They are carried singly, one per stem, so this is a perfect little rose for cutting and arranging. The foliage is shiny rich green, with a burgundy tinge to the new growth that makes an interesting contrast to the pink flowers. As a plant, 'Pierrine' is unusually handsome for a Miniature, reaching just over 2 feet high and nearly as wide, with plenty of leafy covering to provide a setting for the constantly produced blossoms. This is an excellent subject for container gardening, the flower border, or even bedding out. 'Pierrine' is basically healthy, with the occasional disease problem quickly overcome, and if you don't keep it dead-headed it will even produce some interesting little orange-yellow hips. The breeders of this rose hope to introduce an equally fine white sport in the near future.

PINKIE, CLIMBING
Polyantha. Introduced 1952.

The dwarf bush from which this rose sported is a perfectly good variety, but 'Pinkie' hasn't got near the versatility in the garden of 'Climbing Pinkie'. The flowers are the same: huge clusters of coral-pink, semi-double, loose little blossoms with darker veining and a light, sweet fragrance. The foliage is also identical, thick, soft green, and semi-glossy on canes with very few thorns. But the bush, nice as it is, just sits there, while the climbing form has several options. It can be grown very successfully as a cascading shrub, 4 or 5 feet high by 7 feet wide, and is very effective in this form either as a particularly graceful hedge or placed so it will trail the tips of its flowering canes into a garden pond. 'Climbing Pinkie' can also be used as its name suggests, and it will create an outstanding display of lush flowers and foliage when trained onto any support—fence, trellis, or building. This very healthy and vigorous rose puts out a constant supply of new 8- to 12-foot shoots from the base, so the major effort in working with it is to thin out the older canes every year, unless you have space to just let it go.

PRIDE 'N' JOY
Miniature. Introduced 1991.

'Pride 'n' Joy' doesn't have as high a rating from the American Rose Society as 'Pierrine', but the two roses have a lot in common from a gardener's perspective, both being hard-working, healthy little bushes. This rose has nicely scented, very double flowers with elegant, Hybrid Tea-type buds that open a vivid mixed orange and yellow and fade to creamy salmon in the sun. They're produced freely throughout the growing season on a slightly spreading plant that's large for a Miniature, reaching nearly 3 feet in height and equally wide. The foliage is dark green

and semi-glossy, giving good coverage to a well-branched bush. This bright little rose shines in a container garden, but it also has great value in the flower bed. It will work as a footing of complementary color for certain old roses such as the orange-washed 'Comtesse du Cayla', and is equally at home filling in under vivid modern Floribundas like yellow 'Sun Flare' or scarlet 'Showbiz'. Try using 'Pride 'n' Joy' alternately with 'Rise 'n' Shine' for an eye-catching edging.

PROSPERITY
Hybrid Musk. Introduced 1919.

This was a rose that I had to learn to like. I saw it first grown on a pillar fully exposed to the sun, and it seemed bleached out and pretty ordinary. Then some gardening friends decided to put it in their semi-shaded yard, on a tall fence of gray wood and limestone, and the pale blossoms—milk white with a touch of beige at the center—showed how handsome they can be. The fragrant flowers are medium-sized and fully double, borne in large clusters fairly steadily through the growing season. This rose is

modest in size for a Hybrid Musk: if allowed to grow as a shrub it will be about 3 feet high and 4 or 5 feet wide, while as a climber 'Prosperity's' canes stretch to 8 or 10 feet. It's really an excellent pillar rose—if set against a darker background—and an easy-to-manage specimen for training along a trellis or wall. The foliage is olive green, rather dark and very healthy, on a plant that will handle poor soils, heat and if pruned back hard, so that it can eventually form more of a hedge—3 or 4 feet high by 8 feet wide—than a blanket. If you want to keep it low you may have to select for the more prostrate canes and prune away any that start to rise too much. With this kind of grooming it makes a spectacular display trailing from a large container on a balcony. 'Red Cascade' is very easy to start from cuttings and will often layer itself where it touches the soil— the new little plants make great hanging baskets until the rose outgrows them.

REGENSBERG
Floribunda. Introduced 1979.

Breeder Sam McGredy of New Zealand has introduced a whole line of special-colored roses he calls "Hand-Painted." 'Regensberg' is one of the best of these for garden use. The large, cupped, fragrant flowers are semi-double affairs of a dark rose-pink that blends well with the older cultivars, but they're edged with pristine white and have a strong white eye under the gold stamens and a whitish reverse to the petals. Sometimes there will be white streaks as well, or the back petals may be solid white without a spot of pink on them. The compact plant, usually about 2 feet high and wide, is well covered with healthy, glossy, dark green foliage that's divided into serrated and pointed leaflets and is disease resistant even in a fair amount of shade. This is a fine little rose to feature in a container garden, and it's equally useful for edging a bed or for hiding the naked ankles of a taller variety. The color, though soft, is so dramatically marked that 'Regensberg' will even work as a short bedding out plant.

RÊVE D'OR
Noisette. Introduced 1869.

When displayed on an exhibition table, the best flowers of this rose can be confused with the best flowers of the Tea rose, 'Safrano'. They have the same shades of buff and golden apricot and much the same semi-double, open-centered form. One difference is that 'Rêve d'Or' usually has more petals to its flowers, even under stress of hot summer sun, and the fragrance is both stronger and more complex than 'Safrano's' Tea scent. In the garden it's impossible to make a mistake, because the Noisette is a vigorous climber that will reach more than 15 feet in height. Its rich green foliage, shapely and pointed, thoroughly covers the long graceful canes and is rarely bothered by anything except a little blackspot. It's a very good rose to train because the canes are quite flexible when young and only moderately thorny, and it's a versatile size that can be used on a pillar, trellis, archway, or gazebo. 'Rêve d'Or', which means "golden dreams" in French, will also work as a spreading, cascading plant at the edge of a retaining wall or in a whiskey barrel on a balcony. Canes that don't naturally arch over and down can be removed or artificially weighted until they retain the desired form.

RISE 'N' SHINE
Miniature. 1977.

Rather like a valuable stud Chihuahua, little 'Rise 'n' Shine' has donated its sturdy genes to innumerable progeny that have gone on to commercial success. A jewel among its offspring is the exhibition star 'Center Gold', whose flowers are even larger and shapelier than those of its fertile parent. 'Rise 'n' Shine' is a garden stalwart, however, whose adaptability and disease resistance are well proven. This tidy little bush stays between 2 and 3 feet high, producing a constant succession of lightly fragrant clean yellow blooms from high-centered shapely buds. The open flowers can get washed to pale straw by harsh sun, but more are always on the way, and 'Rise 'n' Shine' will tolerate the protection of afternoon shade if you plan to be out looking at your roses at midday in midsummer and want them to be always at their best. The fresh blooms are a bright color that mixes beautifully with some of the "hot" perennials like coreopsis or gallardia, lavender or cream lantana. They can provide a color footing for larger yellow roses such as 'Graham Thomas' or 'Perle des Jardins', and they make an entertaining border mixed with the remontant dwarf yellow daylily, 'Stella d'Oro'.

R. RUGOSA RUBRA
Species. Date of introduction unknown.

Rosa rugosa is an incredibly disease-resistant and cold-hardy member of the Species class, famous for its shining, deeply veined (rugosed) foliage. It's also well known for the thick coating of sharp prickles on the new growth, which earned it the nickname of "Hedgehog Rose," and the large, glossy brick-orange hips, whose similarity to another fruit led to the name "Tomato Rose." The Species type has a number of clones, including the lovely, white-flowered *R. rugosa alba*, but the *R. rugosa rubra* clone has the largest flowers of the group. They are single, with five lightly crinkled petals of shining magenta-purple and a bloom reminiscent of silk. As with most Rugosas, there's a wonderful fragrance of rose mixed with cloves that lingers even when the petals are dried for potpourri. The flowers are produced in waves throughout the growing season, and each flush is followed with fruit, so there will be layers of hips at various stages of maturity all on the bush at the same time. These are some of the best-flavored and most useful of all rose hips for any culinary purpose—they're also tasty straight from the bush. The plant reaches 4 or 5 feet high, and it suckers freely so the width varies by how often you shovel-prune the roots. It's very healthy in most situations but will do much better in the South and live longer if given a light, well-prepared soil with adequate water and mulch to keep the roots cool in summer.

ly as wide, that shows the influence of its Hybrid Musk parent, 'Ballerina', in the open habit of growth. The canes are flexible enough to train fanned out against a wall or fence, if you are worried they'll take too much space from other roses in the garden, but they are beautiful left to billow out on their own. This rose can also be pruned into a more compact shape, so that the flower clusters are closer to the thick foliage of dark, glossy green. 'Sally Holmes' is quite healthy in the garden, with only occasional touches of blackspot, and it's also very successful on the exhibition bench, where the massive and beautiful flower clusters win regular awards.

SARAH VAN FLEET
Hybrid Rugosa. Introduced 1926.

This is one of the two best Hybrid Rugosas for the South, with its white sport, 'Mary Manners', being the other. 'Sarah Van Fleet' was recorded as being the result of a cross between *Rosa rugosa* and a Hybrid Tea, but the chromosome numbers don't match as they should and most rosarians believe that the non-rugosa parent must have been something else. Whatever it was, it works out very well for gardeners who want the beauty of the cold-hardy rugosas in a warm garden. 'Sarah' has large, slightly cupped semi-double flowers with silky petals of warm pink and a rich fragrance that's a little more sweet than spicy. The huge and handsome bush, 6 or 7 feet high by at least 5 feet wide, has remarkably thorny canes well-covered by semi-glossy leathery leaves of medium green. Like most Hybrid Rugosas in the South, this rose can get a little blackspot, but it rarely loses much foliage and it's remarkably tolerant of poor clay soil. 'Sarah Van Fleet' has multiple flushes of bloom in the cool weather of spring and fall, but always has some flowers even in midsummer. It's a good choice for hedging or barrier planting, a backdrop for shorter roses or as a specimen to stand alone in a place of honor.

SEA FOAM
Shrub. Introduced 1964.

'Sea Foam' was produced by crossing the Large-flowered Climber 'White Dawn' (a 'New Dawn' descendant) with the pink Floribunda 'Pinocchio'—three times. Instead of closeset eyes or hemophilia, this multiple inbreeding created a handsome and healthy rose. 'Sea Foam' has medium-large, very double flowers of rich creamy white, produced in clusters along canes covered with glossy, leathery leaves of dark green. The Tea rose fragrance is very strong when they first open, though it quickly fades. The flowers themselves last forever, staying attractive on the plant for as long as two weeks. They don't have very long stems, but a blooming cane can make a dramatic addition to an indoor flower arrangement. One of the best varieties for use as a groundcover, 'Sea Foam' is also a good choice for containers on balconies or beds behind retaining walls—it naturally likes to grow over and down. The rose will mound up to about 3 feet high eventually, with canes that spread 6 feet wide. You can get it to hang even more by training the young canes with decorative bottles or bricks tied to the ends, or you can tie it up instead as a handsome pillar rose. It's a sturdy variety that only occasionally suffers from a little blackspot and is tolerant of most growing conditions.

SEVEN SISTERS
Hybrid Multiflora. Introduced 1817.

This was once an extremely popular rose, and nurserymen must have made capital on the name: there are a number of red or white Floribundas masquerading as 'Seven Sisters' today. The most common variety with which it's confused in my area is 'Eutin', but the two roses have no features in common except the ability to produce roses in clusters. The flowers of the original 'Seven Sisters' are medium-small, very double florets in shades of cream, rose, and crimson, produced in moderate clusters only in the spring. They're not dramatic in appearance, but pleasantly soft and lightly fragrant. The plant is a vigorous climber, with canes that can reach 15 or 20 feet, and it will do very well trained into trees or cascading over high fences. The foliage is the most distinctive feature of the rose to botanists, being comprised of very broad, slightly downy leaflets, with a pair of deeply fringed wings, or stipules, where each leaf joins the cane. The rose was originally described as a separate species, under the name *Rosa multiflora platyphylla*, or "broadleaf multiflora," but it was later thought to be a cultivar selected for the Chinese gardens from whence it came. 'Seven Sisters' is a healthy and interesting rose, not one for a center-stage planting, but a good background plant whose true identity is well worth preserving.

SHAILER'S PROVENCE
Centifolia. Introduced before 1799.

It was on the first-ever South Carolina Rose Rustle (Carolina rosarians may "preserve" or "collect," but they do not "rustle" unless Texans are present) that Ruth Knopf introduced me to this rose. It was growing on the grounds of a privately-owned plantation house, held by the same family for more than two centuries, not far from a swimming pool with a Greek statue in one end. There were other wonderful roses there as well, "collected" by the current owner's mother, but none of them were as unbelievably fragrant as 'Shailer's Provence'. The flowers are good-sized cups, borne usually in clusters of three and absolutely crammed with layers of tissue-thin lilac-pink petals. They smother the whole plant in spring, being produced at almost every axillary bud along the relaxed canes that arch and drape the ground under their perfumed weight. The foliage is a soft, matte gray-green, elegantly beautiful with the old-fashioned blossoms, and it's very healthy throughout the spring blooming season. 'Shailer's Provence' mounds up about 4 feet high and 5 feet wide if left to itself. The only pruning ever needed is to remove dead or damaged material, because you won't want to cut away any of the flowering potential of this once-blooming rose. Faults are a tendency to shed some foliage in a sort of summer dormancy, and the flowers will ball if the buds get caught in the rain. The bloom season is long enough to supply a good show even with some losses, however, and 'Shailer's Provence' is remarkably tolerant of clay soils and heat well into zone 8.

pale, flesh pink petals are exquisitely formed and arranged, as if an artist in porcelain flowers had adjusted them to have maximum effect on the human eye. The fragrance is as powerful as the original, but the tolerance for dampness is greater; balling is not a problem at all. Of all their class, these two "Souvenirs" are nearly the most floriferous and disease resistant for a warm climate—only the found Bourbon, "Maggie," can beat them as a garden-worthy plant.

SPARRIESHOOP
Shrub. Introduced 1953.

A Gold Medal winner in Portland in 1971, this big Shrub rose remains a strong favorite more than forty years after its introduction. The flowers are large, 4 inches across, with five wavy light pink petals unfurling from a long and pointed bud to show a frothy cluster of gold stamens. The fragrance varies, being much stronger when the petals first open and more noticeable on a warm day than a cool one. The blossoms are produced in heavy flushes both in spring and fall, with few flowers in the summer. 'Sparrieshoop' is supposed to be a 5-foot-high bush, but for Southern gardeners it's more likely to try for 7 feet tall and 4 or 5 feet wide, with a good covering of thick, shiny, dark green foliage. This rose is quite disease resistant in most locations, including some shade, so it's a good choice for a specimen or hedge plant, or a deep green backdrop for bright summer flowers. When in bloom the flowers make a long-lasting display on the bush, and they also last remarkably well in cut arrangements for indoors.

SPICE
Found China? No date of introduction.

One of the Bermuda Mystery Roses, this lovely foundling shows traits of both the China and Tea classes, but leans more towards the China in its compact growth habit. The flowers, cupped and loosely double, are the softest shade of pink, fading to creamy white as they age in the sun. It has been suggested that this is really one of the very first of the roses brought West from China, a variety known since 1809 as 'Hume's Blush Tea-Scented China'. This could be quite possible, given the combination of Bermuda's climate—perfect for Teas and Chinas—and its long history as a haven for sailing ships trading around the world. Island gardeners, however, have christened it for the intense, distinctive fragrance and know it familiarly and simply as "Spice." What appears to be the same rose has also been found in old Southern cemeteries, including one in Natchez, Mississippi and several in Texas. Wherever it grows it shows a tendency to perform well under stressful conditions, blooming constantly and keeping a good covering of medium green foliage. The bush usually reaches 3 to 4 feet high and nearly as wide. In my garden it is one of the most disease free of all roses.

STAR DELIGHT
Hybrid Rugosa. Introduced 1990.

This nifty new variety from breeder Ralph Moore has every quality of toughness for which its class is known, only compressed into a smaller form. He's introduced it as an "Americana Rose," perhaps to make the point that British rose breeder David Austin, with his "English" roses is not the only producer of fine new garden plants. The dainty flowers are single, covering the bush with a profusion of neat, dark, rose-pink blossoms, each showing a starburst of gold stamens backed by a bright white eye. The petals are separated and pointed, so the flowers do look like vivid little stars. Fragrance is minimal—unusual in a Hybrid Rugosa—but there is a light scent when the flowers first open. The bush is wonderful, a compact 3-foot-high-and-wide plant densely covered with healthy, dark, olive-green foliage. The combination with the showy little flowers is quite striking, and this rose would make an excellent specimen for display in a large container. It can also be clipped into a neat, regularly blooming hedge. 'Star Delight' is both very cold hardy and very tolerant of Southern soils and climate conditions.

STARINA
Miniature. Introduced 1965.

This old variety—old for a Miniature—remains one of the top exhibition Mini's in the country with an "almost perfect" ARS rating of 9.0 and several prestigious awards to its credit. It's also a lasting favorite both with growers and with gardeners. The double, beautifully-shaped flowers are a bright orange-scarlet that shows up at quite a distance. They have only a slight fragrance, most detectable just as the blossoms begin to open. This is one of the first Miniature roses to bloom in the spring, and one of the steadiest repeaters throughout the long growing season. 'Starina' has a good garden form as well, with a neatly compact little bush about 2 feet high that stays well covered with foliage. The leaves are proportionately small, glossy and dark green, with very good disease resistance. This is a rose that can perform well in any landscape setting, as a bright little edging plant, or in a container. It also makes an excellent cut flower for indoor arrangements.

SUN FLARE
Floribunda. Introduced 1981.

Yellow roses, in the language of flowers, signify jealousy, infidelity, and decrease of love, but they are very beautiful in the garden. This prime example is a descendent of the equally worthy 'Sunsprite', a Kordes Floribunda introduced in 1977. Both roses are healthy and floriferous, with 'Sun Flare' having a slight edge in petal count. Both are also fragrant, which is rare in modern yellow roses. The books say that the parent rose has the best scent, but I've found the licorice fragrance of 'Sun Flare' to be equally strong and more consistently noticeable, which is probably why I prefer it. The bright flowers are medium in size, borne in clusters of three or more consistently throughout the growing season. The very shapely buds open wide at maturity to show stamens that are first yellow and then

and loaded, by autumn, with equally tiny red hips—it's a great choice. The little, semi-double blossoms are musky-scented, and their aroma is detectable from a fair distance when the plant is in heavy bloom. The hips are not only colorful, but good bird food—about the size of dogwood berries. Birds that might balk at the size of the fruits on 'Hansa', for example, can easily handle these. They also have the option with 'Trier' of dining at home, because it's a favorite rose for nesting. The thorny canes reach 8 to 12 feet long and can be trained after the fashion of a climbing rose, but the plant is really too vigorous and too well-armed to make this an enticing proposition. As a specimen left to mound up and naturalize, 'Trier' is ideal—it tolerates all sorts of soils and any kind of weather, and will gradually become a prime wildlife sanctuary. This is one of the best roses for making a gradual visual transition between the intense color of a flower garden and the quieter view of surrounding woods or countryside.

TROPICANA
Hybrid Tea. Introduced 1960.

This rose is supposed to be afflicted by powdery mildew, but it is hard to actually hurt and remains very popular with gardeners. I've seen its soft coral-orange flowers—sort of caviar-colored—in yards and cemeteries across the South, both in situations where it gets loving care and others where it receives total neglect. It seems to be one of the toughest of Hybrid Teas available. 'Tropicana' also has at least five rose awards behind its name and still wins occasionally on the exhibition bench. The flowers are large and well-formed, unfurling from pointed buds to high-centered shapely blossoms. The fragrance is pretty good, too, more fruity than Tealike. The bush gets 3 or 4 feet tall, with the narrow shape and stiff, erect canes of a typical Hybrid Tea. The foliage is dark green, leathery and glossy, and only moderately abundant—also fairly typical. 'Tropicana' is not a color that blends easily with the blue-pink range of roses, but it goes like a dream with dark red, white, or shades of yellow. A grouping of Miniature roses, such as 'Rise 'n' Shine' and 'Millie Walters', around the bottom of the bush will help to hide any bareness there and bring out the best in this old favorite.

VALENTINE
Floribunda. Introduced 1951.

It was as a rustled rose that I first came to know this plant. Mike Shoup of The Antique Rose Emporium had given it the study name of "Fabulous," partly because of its constant production of flowers, and partly because his work crew accidentally bush-hogged a planting of it that had been hidden by high weeds (we grow 'em tall in Texas). The roses didn't die, but cheerfully went ahead and bloomed at their new 2 inch height—the sort of positive behavior that wins friends and influences people. I still think Mike's name was more representative than the name under which this rose was finally identified, in spite of the color of the blossoms. The flowers are medium-sized, semi-double, bright red on the inside and lighter on the reverse of the petals. They are carried in relaxed clusters on a bush that is compact and nicely shaped, and usually well covered with rich green, semi-glossy foliage. 'Valentine' has no fragrance to speak of, but it also has no problems. It will tolerate any growing conditions, handle miserably hot weather, and even thrive in partial shade. It's a truly ideal landscape plant, and the slight droop of its flowers gives it a softer look than many other Floribundas, so it also blends well with older roses in the garden.

VEILCHENBLAU
Hybrid Multiflora. Introduced 1909.

If you don't mind the guttural name, this is one of the most delightful climbing roses in the landscape, primarily because of the color. The individual flowers are small, blue-purple with some white streaks and a tiny white center accented by bright golden stamens. They are borne in huge clusters, however, because this rose only blooms once a year so it has to put all its reproductive energy into one massive burst. Trained up a trellis near lilac bushes, or spread out on a wall behind those tall, old-fashioned "black" purple hollyhocks, nothing could be more royal. One year I planted shiny purple cabbages around the base of the plant to carry the same color through all the levels: they were fat and gorgeous when the rose bloomed in early spring. 'Veilchenblau' is fragrant, too, with a strong scent of green apples mixed with a little musk. The plant is not as rampant as some of its multiflora cousins; the canes are usually only about 10 or 12 feet long, not too numerous to handle for training, and, best of all, nearly thornless. The foliage is a light matte green, with long, graceful leaflets. 'Veilchenblau' is reasonably tolerant of most growing conditions, but it will live longest and bloom most heavily in a well-prepared, well-drained soil.

VINCENT GODSIFF
China. Date of introduction unknown.

In Bermuda, where this rose was collected, it blooms straight through pretty much twelve months of the year. They have no frosts to slow it down, and it has the stamina to mount display after display of luminous dark pink flowers with no risk of exhaustion. Because it isn't likely that this variety will ever be properly identified, it has now been reregistered under its island study name and formally reintroduced to commerce as 'Vincent Godsiff'. It would be a shame to miss out on a rose this good just for lack of a proper identity. The semi-double, open-centered flowers have no scent, but they are visible from a great distance, almost neon-bright on the compact 3-foot-high bush. The very healthy foliage is neatly pointed in the typical China fashion, and covers the plant thickly. This is a truly fine landscape rose, one that will tolerate poor conditions and rejoice in good ones, blooming constantly from spring to late fall. Though it's legally an Old Garden Rose, 'Vincent Godsiff' is almost too bright to put near some of the pastel pinks. It mixes well with stronger colors, even with some of the more shocking modern roses, and this rose looks particularly at home with vivid perennials around and behind it.

WHITE MEIDILAND
Shrub. Introduced 1986.

This is perhaps the best of the light-colored Meidiland groundcover roses for the South. The white flowers, blushing faintly pink at times, are quite large, flat, and very double. They form heavy clusters along the trailing canes in the spring and there's a pretty good repeat bloom in the fall. If stimulated by a little light grooming, this rose may even produce scattered flowers during the summer, but that feature isn't reliable in a warm climate. If left unsprayed the rose can defoliate periodically, but this genuinely doesn't affect its vigor, and the leaves come back fresh in a short period of time. 'White Meidiland' has its biggest advantage over the 'Alba' and 'Pearl' cultivars because of its behavior in the garden: it stays where you plant it, mounding to a few feet high and spreading about 6 feet across. The other two cultivars root wherever they touch ground—great if you're looking for erosion control or a highway embankment planting, but not so handy in limited space. Grown in combination with perennials, such as soft blue *Salvia farinacea*, any summer faults are covered and 'White Meidiland' is a beautiful addition to a flowering border. It also looks good trailing over the top of a stone-walled embankment or draping down the sides of a large container.

WINSOME
Miniature. 1984.

I grew 'Winsome' for three years in an old clawfoot bathtub, with two other roses and some irises on a balcony exposed to all-day direct sun, reflected light, hot wind from the air conditioner and temperatures that varied much more widely and rapidly than those on the ground, 15 feet below. The same plant has now been transferred into a regular garden bed, where it's gained 6 inches in height out of sheer relief and doubled the number of leaves it can carry. It bloomed fairly well for me even under broiler-oven conditions, with beautifully shaped reddish-mauve flowers that look great in a lapel vase and dry a nice dark color for potpourri. The flowers are not listed as fragrant, but they often have a very sweet scent when first open—it would be better to credit them with a variable perfume, I think.

'Winsome' has an excellent reputation for disease resistance in a normal garden setting, with rather glossy dark green foliage on a bushy, compact plant that gets 2 to 3 feet tall. It does well in borders of mixed Mini's, as a colorful accent in a herb garden or settled near the foot of a larger rose. It's a good choice for containers (obviously), though orange clay pots are a little at odds with the flower color, unless you go all the way and underplant 'Winsome' with orange and purple 'Jolly Joker' pansies.

YVONNE RABIER
Polyantha. Introduced 1910.

Sometimes the flowers will attract you to a rose, sometimes the form of the plant or the richness of the foliage, rarely are they all in such perfect balance as with this little bush. The flowers are small, but not too small, double, and gathered in clusters of baptismal white with only a hint of yellow at the center behind the yellow stamens. They decorate a plant that is slightly spreading, reaching about 3 feet in every direction and thoroughly covered with rough, glossy green foliage. The flowers are constantly produced through the growing season, but they have almost no fragrance—and the combination of white clusters on a green bush is not so unusual. It's hard to explain why this rose is so particularly pleasing until you've measured its proportions with your own eye. 'Yvonne Rabier' is quite useful as well as aesthetically satisfying; it's a good size for a container garden on a deck, and it will also fit into the flower bed with no trouble. It can be pruned as a low hedge or included in a white garden, but it would be really fine as the centerpiece of an herb garden, where the clean scent of herbs would enhance the clean beauty of the rose.

ZÉPHIRINE DROUHIN
Bourbon. Introduced 1868.

If virtue can be combined with beauty to produce a rose, this is it. Large, loosely-double flowers of intense pink color and gorgeous scent are produced in free profusion on this vigorous, but thornless, climber. Except for a few prickles on the bottoms of the leaf petioles, there are no sharp objects on the entire plant, and no blood to be lost when grooming and training it. 'Zéphirine Drouhin', like most climbing roses, needs about three years to get properly established and reach its full powers of blooming. After that it is one of the most floriferous of the Bourbons for the South.

The canes reach 10 to 12 feet, making this a moderately sized climber, and they are quite flexible and easy to train on pillar or trellis. The new growth is beautiful, a deep burgundy color that contrasts strongly with the pink flowers. So many new canes are produced each year that it can be necessary to undo the plant and remove half to two-thirds of the older growth annually—something to take into account when deciding on its position in the garden design. Because of the lack of prickles, 'Zéphirine Drouhin' is ideal for public plantings and archways or arbors where passersby might run the risk of getting snagged. It can even be pruned to about 6 feet high and grown as a large shrub in areas unsuitable for climbers. The rose will tolerate a variety of growing conditions, but like most Bourbons it will do best in good soil. It gets some blackspot, but not too much, and sets some hips, though not too many.

ORGANIC ROSES: THE AFTERTASTE

A rose is a rose is a tea, a dessert, a salad, a soup . . . You want romantic? You are what you eat, so for a rose lover you can't get more intimately connected. You want practical? Roses have been valued medicinally, nutritionally, and therapeutically for millennia. There are reams of ancient recipes for edibles and medicinals using roses, probably more than any other single flower. Even today you can't get pass a pharmacy or beauty counter without seeing roses in their traditional places: rose-scented soap, astringent rose water for facial toning, Vitamin C with rose hips, etc. Rose oil remains one of the top ingredients in modern perfumes. The only place roses have lost any ground is in the kitchen, and even that's not true across the board. In the Middle East and the Orient, numerous dishes call for rose water, dried rose buds, and more, while residents of Scandinavia have never abandoned their flavorful rose hip soup. There is a reason why everything from deer to Japanese beetles wants to eat your roses—they're good food.

Since pesticide-free roses are the essential ingredient of every rose product from tea to potpourri, an organic rose garden is a natural production plant for flavorful or fragrant products. If you try the following recipes, do not use any rose petals or rose hips from chemically treated plants. Even if you've used insecticidal soap, wait at least a few days and wash the plants thoroughly before using them!

ABOUT ROSE PETALS

Rose petals, also called rose "leaves" in many old recipes, contain quercitrin, volatile perfume oils, and natural coloring agents. Their astringency makes them useful in decoctions prescribed for sores in the mouth and throat. American Indians reportedly used crushed rose petals combined with bear grease both as a salve for sores and as a scented hair pomade, and soaked the petals in rainwater to make a bath for sore eyes. The perfume of rose flowers in general is supposed to be soothing, bringing harmony to the mind and aiding meditation and sleep. It's also used to help reduce fear and increase vitality in aromatherapy. Strong concentrations of rose scent, however, can give some folks a headache, even trigger migraines in those who are sensitive. At least one king forbade roses to be used in palace flower arrangements for this reason. Since different varieties of roses contain different combinations of aromatic oils in their petals, most people can find at least some kinds whose scent they like and will be comfortable using in food products.

I've often seen instructions to remove the white heel of each rose petal before using it, with the notation that this portion of the petal is bitter. This seemed like a huge amount of picky, time-consuming hand labor, so at first I just blithely disregarded it and hoped my results wouldn't be too bad. As I got more proficient at dealing with floral cookery, it finally occurred to me to test the petals to see if all of them had this bitter heel. Honestly, I can't tell. Raw rose petals to me taste slightly astringent all over. I can't discern the shadings of flavor between differently colored areas. It may be that some of the heaviest, stiffest petals, such as those of some or the heftier Hybrid Teas and Hybrid Perpetuals, have these bitter bits. I wouldn't choose those to cook with anyway, as they'd be tougher to chew. On roses that have light, silky petals like most of the Rugosas, Chinas, and Damasks, clipping is probably not worth the effort, and Miniature rose petals are so small it would drive anyone crazy to handle each one. If you're in any doubt, nibble on the heels of some of the petals you plan to use and see for yourself if they're bitter enough to need trimming.

When collecting petals for food, try to get them in the morning from flowers that are just opening. This way they'll have the maximum amount of perfume oil still intact. Rinse them as you would any produce and dry them in a salad

flavorful. Others, such as 'Old Blush' and 'Dortmund', are fairly tasty and can be successfully used in cooking.

In order to prepare hips for culinary purposes, pick them when newly ripe—plump, crisp and colored orange or red, depending upon the habit of the variety—slice off the blossom end and the stem end, split them open (or quarter them if that's easier) and scrape out the hairy achenes and seeds. Rinse them thoroughly and shake dry in a colander. If you're not going to use them right away, they can be dried on screens in a warm place out of direct light or in a food dryer. As with rose petals, avoid using aluminum for cooking.

Roses for Hips

Rosa canina	*Rosa rugosa rubra*	Hansa
Old Blush	Dortmund	

ℛOSE HIP TEA

1 ¼ cups water
1 heaping tablespoon dried hips or 2 tablespoons fresh, cleaned hips

Bring the water to a boil, pour it over the hips, cover, and let steep for at least 15 minutes. Strain the tea through double-folded cheesecloth to remove any achenes along with the pulp. Add brown sugar or honey to taste. I like this tea much better with a cinnamon stick steeped in it and a squeeze of lemon juice. The steeping doesn't get as much flavor from the hips as longer cooking does, and the tea, while very good for you, can be a little bland.

Rose hip tea has traditionally been used for all sorts of internal complaints, from gonorrhea and yeast infections to glaucoma. It's probably effective for mild bladder infections, and at the very least it's completely non-toxic and loaded with vitamin C.

ℛOSE HIP SOUP

2 cups dried rose hips, presoaked in 2 cups water (or 3 cups fresh, cleaned hips)
4½ cups water (4 cups if using fresh hips)

½ cup turbinado (raw) sugar or ¼ cup honey
1 tablespoon cornstarch

Soak dried rose hips overnight in 2 cups of water; they will absorb all of it. Bring the 4½ cups water to a boil in a stainless steel saucepan and add the rose hips. Let the mixture return to a boil, then lower the temperature and simmer for 20 minutes until the hips are soft and pulpy. Remove from heat and strain through a sieve lined with cheesecloth to clean achenes, seeds, and stem bits from final product. (Keep the pulp for making jelly, or feed it (cool) to the chickens or add to compost heap.)

Add the sugar or honey to the rose hip liquid and reheat, stirring, until the sweetener is completely dissolved. Mix a small amount of the liquid with the cornstarch in a separate bowl, then stir the cornstarch into the hot liquid. Bring to a low boil, stirring constantly, until the mixture has thickened, about 2 minutes. Makes about 4 cups of soup.

Rose hip soup can be served hot before the entree, garnished with sour cream, or cold at the end of the meal, garnished with whipped cream (flavored with 1 teaspoon sugar and 2 teaspoons rose water instead of vanilla) and chopped pecans. It's tart and flavorful, has a texture like smooth warm honey and is sort of a reddish-brown, burnt sienna color that's really pretty in the right bowls.

*R*OSE HIP SAUCE

4 cups (1 quart) water
2 cups dried rose hips, pre-soaked (or 3 cups fresh, cleaned hips)
½ cup sugar or ¼ cup honey

Bring water to a boil, add hips and simmer for 2 hours, or until the pulp is very soft. Strain the thick mixture through a large sieve, mashing the hips to get as much pulp as possible. Sweeten the warm sauce to taste. Let it cool, then store in the refrigerator in a closed container. It will keep for several weeks.

If you reduce the amount of water for rose hip soup you get this thicker, pulpier sauce that is a little lower in Vitamin C (because of the longer cooking time) but rich in flavor and remarkably versatile. It will replace apple butter, or can be used for a topping over ice cream or brandied pears and goes great with yogurt and granola. Rose hip sauce can be used instead of prunes or raisins or most other cooked fruits in any recipe. It can also be used to fill desert tarts. Sophisticated variations include adding ginger, cloves, nutmeg or cinnamon, and a little brandy, Grand Marnier, or orange liqueur.

paste is workably thick, let the mixture cool. (Cast iron is important because it affects the color of the paste, turning it blackish red. This is the one time it's good to use a metal other than stainless steel in contact with cooking roses. If you cook the petal mixture down in a regular saucepan you get an odd brownish paste that's not nearly as attractive.)

Form the beads by hand-rolling evenly sized balls of paste. Make the balls twice the size you want for the finished beads: they shrink 50% while drying. Stick a pin through the center of each bead as you finish rolling it and pin all of them into a piece of cardboard or Styrofoam for drying—if you don't pre-pierce them they can crumble when you try to do it later. Move each bead up and down on its pin every day or so to prevent sticking. Drying takes about a week, then the dark fragrant beads are ready to string and wear. Making rose beads is a slow process overall, but the effort involved is not great—most of it is spent simply waiting.

If you don't have enough rose petals to make a complete string, or if you want them to go farther, other beads (such as gold, silver, amethyst, etc.) can be strung with them. These beads, and clasps of different kinds, can be found at craft shops or through mail-order catalogs. You can also use these other beads as markers if you're making your rose beads into a rosary, one of the most traditional uses.

Body heat brings out the fragrance of rose beads; the scent is more intense against the naked skin. If the rose petals used were not very fragrant, a few drops of rose water added to the cooled cooked paste will increase the scent. Storing the beads in a sealed container in the refrigerator between wearings will preserve the aromatic oils for an exceptionally long time.

CAREFREE "POTPOURRI"

I'm not a regular potpourri maker because, while I like potpourri, you can't eat it or wear it, you have to dust the pretty containers, and on the whole I prefer the scent of fresh roses. I do have a compromise tactic, however, to avoid wasting the fragrant petals and bits of herbs collected on almost every trip around the garden. I've learned to keep a colander (ceramic ones are the prettiest; once again, avoid aluminum or any metal except stainless steel) by the kitchen door and drop my gatherings in it. The holes help keep the changing mixture aerated to avoid fungus, and it also gets stirred by hand daily as I add petals or just fluff it to enjoy the rich fragrances. As the plant material dries out I add it to the compost and start over. This way you don't get the beautiful appearance of a proper potpourri, or the specific lasting scent that careful drying in combination with a fixative provides, but you get the more intense scents of the fresh flowers and herbs (and citrus peel from the kitchen), changing in complexity while they dry.

RESOURCES

$\mathscr{P}$UBLICATIONS OF INTEREST

Combined Rose List 1996, compiled and edited by Beverly R. Dobson and Peter Schneider. This essential, annually updated resource lists the roses available in commerce and where to find them. Cost is $18, from: Peter Schneider, P.O. Box 677, Mantua, OH 44255.

Modern Roses 10, published by the American Rose Society, is a hardcover listing with descriptions of "roses of historical and botanical importance including all modern international rose registrations." It is current to 1993. Available from the American Rose Society, P.O. Box 30,000, Shreveport, LA 71130-0030. (318) 938-5402.

$\mathscr{B}$OOKS OF INTEREST

Antique Roses for the South. William C. Welch. Dallas, TX: Taylor Publishing Company, 1991.

Climbing Roses. Stephen Scanniello and Tania Bayard. New York, NY: Prentice Hall, 1994.

Common Sense Pest Control. Olkowski and Daar. Newtown, CT: Taunton Press, 1991.

Compost This Book! Tom Christopher and Marty Asher. San Francisco, CA: Sierra Club Books, 1994.

David Austin's English Roses. David Austin. Little, Brown and Company, 1993.

Easy Care Roses. Stephen Scanniello, Editor. Brooklyn, NY: Brooklyn Botanic Garden, 1995.

Gardening Success with Difficult Soils. Scott Ogden. Dallas, TX: Taylor Publishing Company, 1992.

Good Neighbors: Companion Planting for Gardeners. Anna Carr. Emmaus, PA: Rodale Press, 1985.

Hardy Roses. Robert Osborne. Pownal, VT: Storey Communications, 1991.

Landscaping with Antique Roses. Liz Druitt and G. Michael Shoup. Newtown, CT: Taunton Press, 1992.

Miniature Roses— Their Care and Cultivation. Sean McCann. Harrisburg, PA: Stackpole Books, 1991.

Modern Garden Roses. Peter Harkness. Chester, CT: The Globe Pequot Press, 1987.

Perennial Garden Color. William C. Welch. Dallas, TX: Taylor Publishing Company, 1989.

Rosa Rugosa. Suzanne Verrier. Deer Park, WI: Capability's Books, 1991.

Roses. Peter Beales. New York, NY: Henry Holt & Company, 1992.

Roses. Roger Phillips and Martyn Rix. New York, NY: Random House, 1988.

The Mini-Rose Garden
P.O. Box 203
Cross Hill, SC 29332
1-800-996-4647
Catalog free.
Mail-order and retail. Miniature roses,
container-grown, all own-root.
Miniatures are rarely contaminated by
virus. Not organic at this time.

Nor'East Miniature Roses Inc.
P.O. Box 307
Rowley, MA 01969
1-800-426-6485
Catalog free.
Mail-order and on-site retail. Miniature
roses, container-grown, all own-root
except for budded standards.
Miniatures are rarely contaminated by
virus. Not organic at this time.

Pickering Nurseries, Inc.
670 Kingston Road
Pickering, Ontario L1V 1A6
Canada
Catalog $4
Mail-order and on-site retail. Modern,
antique, and rare roses budded mostly
on *R. multiflora* rootstock. Growers outside the United States rarely have virus
problems. Offer 800 varieties. No
import permit required.

Pixie Treasures
4121 Prospect Avenue
Yorba Linda, CA 92686
(714) 993-6780
Catalog $1
Mail-order and on-site retail. Miniature
roses, container-grown, all own-root.
Miniatures are rarely contaminated by
virus. Using some organic techniques.

The Rose Ranch
P.O. Box 10087
Salinas, CA 93912
(408) 758-6965
Catalog $3, availability list free
Mail-order primarily. Old, rare, and
selected modern roses, all container-
grown, most own-root. Very virus-
conscious. Using some organic
techniques.

The Roseraie at Bayfields
The Roseraie, Inc.
P.O. Box R
Waldoboro, ME 04572
(207) 832-6330
Catalog free, color video supplement $6
Mail-order and retail. All northern
(zone 5), field-grown, hardy roses, both
own-root and grafted on seedling *R.
canina* and *R. multiflora* to reduce risk of
virus. No spraying, actively involved in
using organic techniques.

Roses Unlimited
Route 1, Box 587
North Deer Wood Drive
Laurens, SC 29360
(803) 682-7673
SASE for availability list
Mail-order primarily. Antique and some
modern roses, own-root, and container-
grown. Have a number of early AARS
winners available. Actively involved in
virus eradication program. Not organic
at this time.

Royall River Roses,
Forevergreen Farm
70 New Gloucester Road
North Yarmouth, ME 04097
(207) 829-5830
Catalog $3
Mail-order and on-site retail. Field-
grown hardy roses, both own-root and
grafted on seedling rootstock, primarily
R. multiflora. Virus conscious. Using
organic growing techniques whenever
possible.

Sequoia Nursery,
Moore Miniature Roses
2519 East Noble Avenue
Visalia, CA 93292
(209) 732-0190

Catalog free.
Mail-order and on-site retail. Miniature
roses, some old and rare varieties, some
Shrub roses. All container-grown and all
own-root except Miniature tree roses.
Most plants offered for sale are propagated from varieties developed on-site
by Ralph Moore, so not subject to virus
infection. Not organic at this time.

Texas Mini-Roses
P.O. Box 267
Denton, TX 76202
(817) 566-3034
Catalog free.
All mail-order. Miniature roses, container-grown, all own-root. Miniatures are
rarely contaminated by virus. Using
some organic techniques.

Vintage Gardens
3003 Pleasant Hill Road
Sebastopol, CA 95472
(707) 829-2035
Availability list free, descriptive catalog
$5
Mail-order and on-site retail. Own-root,
container-grown antique and extraordinary roses, including unique selection
of early Hybrid Teas. Actively involved
in preservation and re-introduction of
"found" roses. 1996 catalog contains
descriptions of 2,000 varieties; custom
propagation orders welcome. Actively
involved in virus eradication program,
practice and promote organic cultivation methods.

SELECTED
ENVIRONMENTAL
SUPPLY SOURCES

Many rose and seed catalogs also offer
organic fertilizers, soil amendments,
and beneficial insects.
Arbico
P.O. Box 4247 CRB
Tucson, AZ 85738-1247

1-800-827-2847
Mail-order catalog offers a wide range
of beneficial insects and biological controls, traps, and monitoring equipment
plus fungal controls, tools, soil care
products, cover crop seeds, and pet
products. They offer consulting service
at (602) 825-9785.

Biofac, Inc.
Beneficial Insects & More
P.O. Box 87
Mathis, TX 78368
1-800-233-4914
Informative catalog explains habits and
uses of the beneficial insects they offer.

Bozeman Bio-Tech
1612 Gold Avenue
P.O. Box 3146
Bozeman, MT 59772
1-800-289-6656
Mail-order catalog includes all forms of
insect controls from traps to biological
and botanical pesticides to beneficial
insects. Also offers some sprayers and
seed spreaders, plus pet products.

Gardeners Supply Company
128 Intervale Road
Burlington, VT 05401
1-800-444-6417
Mail-order catalog offers wide variety of
equipment for seed starting, composting, home greenhouses, yard tools
(including spiked lawn aerator sandals),
trellising materials, plus some organic
soil amendments and mechanical and
biological pest controls.

Gardens Alive!
5100 Schenley Place
Lawrenceburg, IN 47025
(812) 537-8650
Cheerful catalog offers their own organic fertilizer formulations plus regular soil
amendments, beneficial insects, biological and mechanical pest controls and
application equipment, pet products.

The Natural Gardener, Inc.,
Garden-Ville of Austin
8648 Old Bee Caves Road
Austin, TX 78735
(512) 288-6115
Mail-order catalog offers organic fertilizers, cover crop seeds, books, tools,
beneficial insects, biological controls,
organic pesticides, pet products. Retail
location in Texas.

Nitron Industries, Inc.
4605 Johnson Road
P.O. Box 1447
Fayetteville, AR 72702
1-800-835-0123
Mail-order catalog offers their own
organic fertilizer formulations, including several for roses, plus individual
organic fertilizer elements, some pest
control products, and some beneficial
insects.

Peaceful Valley Farm Supply
P.O. Box 2209
Grass Valley, CA 95945
(916) 272-4769
Mail-order and retail, they offer everything you need. Organic amendments,
cover crop seeds, vegetable seeds,
flower bulbs, every variety of natural
pest management, pet products, growing and propagating supplies, garden
tools, farm equipment and books—plus
soil and plant tissue analysis.

Real Goods
966 Mazzoni St.
Ukiah, CA 95482-3471
1-800-762-7325
Mail-order catalog contains products to
complement the organic lifestyle,
including push and rechargeable electric lawnmowers, natural garden pest
controls, bat houses, solar outdoor
lights.

Rincon-Vitova Insectaries, Inc.
P.O. Box 1555
Ventura, CA 93002
1-800-248-2847
Mail-order catalog offers beneficial
insects, seeds and/or seedlings for
plants that support beneficials, and
related books.

Worm's Way
3151 South Highway 446
Bloomington, IN 47401-9111
1-800-274-9676
Wide range of environmentally sound
mail-order products, from organic fertilizers and pest controls to garden lighting, beer making, mushroom growing,
and bird feeders. Retail locations in
Indiana, Florida, Massachusetts, and
Missouri.

BIBLIOGRAPHY

Affleck, Thomas. *1851 and 1852 Catalogue of Fruit and Ornamental Trees and Plants Cultivated at The Southern Nurseries, Washington, Adams County, Mississippi.* (from Louisiana State University collection).

Affleck, Thomas. *Affleck's Southern Rural Almanac, and Plantation and Garden Calendar for 1860.* Brenham, TX: The New Year's Creek Settler's Association. 1986 reprint.

The American Rose Society. (Haring, Peter A., ed.). *Modern Roses 9.* Shreveport, LA: The American Rose Society. 1986.

The American Rose Society. (Cairns, Thomas, ed.). *Modern Roses 10.* Shreveport, LA: The American Rose Society. 1993.

Austin, David. *David Austin's English Roses.* Little, Brown and Company. 1993.

Bailey, Liberty Hyde, and Bailey, Ethel Zoe. *Hortus Third.* New York, NY: Macmillan. 1976.

Beales, Peter. *Classic Roses.* New York, NY: Holt Rinehart & Winston. 1985.

Beales, Peter. *Roses.* New York, NY: Henry Holt & Company. 1992.

Beales, Peter. *Twentieth Century Roses.* New York, NY: Harper & Row. 1988.

The Bermuda Rose Society. *Old Garden Roses in Bermuda.* Bermuda: The Bermuda Rose Society. 1984.

Borchard, Ruth. *Oh My Own Rose.* Self-published. 1982.

Carr, Anna. *Good Neighbors: Companion Planting for Gardeners.* Emmaus, PA: Rodale Press. 1985.

Christopher, Tom and Asher, Marty. *Compost This Book!* San Francisco, CA: Sierra Club Books. 1994.

Dobson, Beverly and Schneider, Peter. *Combined Roses List 1995.* Mantua, OH: self-published.

Drennan, Georgia Torrey. *Everblooming Roses.* New York, NY: Duffield & Company. 1912.

Druitt, Liz and Shoup, Michael. *Landscaping with Antique Roses.* Newtown, CT: The Taunton Press. 1992.

Earle, Alice Morse. *Old Time Gardens.* New York, NY: The Macmillan Company. 1901.

Ellefson, Connie, Tom Stephens, and Doug Welsh. *Xeriscape Gardening.* New York, NY: Macmillan Publishing. 1992.

Evans, Augusta Jane. *St. Elmo.* Alpharetta, GA: Seven Stars. 1866 (facsimile reproduction).

Fisher, John. *The Companion To Roses.* Topsfield, MA: Salem House. 1987.

Harkness, Peter. *Modern Garden Roses.* Chester, CT: The Globe Pequot Press. 1987.

Hole, S. Reynolds. *A Book about Roses.* London, Great Britain: Edward Arnold. 1896.

Horst, R. Kenneth. *Compendium of Rose Diseases.* St. Paul, MN: The American Phytopathological Society and Cornell University. 1983.

Lawrence, Elizabeth. *Through the Garden Gate.* Chapel Hill, NC: The University of North Carolina Press. 1990.

Le Rougetel, Hazel. *A Heritage of Roses.* Owings Mills, Maryland: Stemmer House. 1988.

Leighton, Ann. *American Gardens of the Nineteenth Century.* Amherst, MA: University of Massachusetts Press. 1987.

McCain, Larry. *Compost: Gardener's Gold.* Washington, TX: Peaceable Kingdom School. 1993.

McCann, Sean. *Miniature Roses—Their Care and Cultivation.* Harrisburg, PA: Stackpole Books. 1991.

McKeon, Judith C. *The Encyclopedia of Roses.* Emmaus, PA: Rodale Press, Inc. 1995.

McMahon, Bernard. *The American Gardener's Calendar.* Philadelphia, PA: B. Graves. 1806 (facsimile edition).

Meilland, Alain. *A Life in Roses.* Carbondale and Edwardsville, IL: Southern Illinois University Press. 1984 ed. of 1969 work.

Ogden, Scott. *Gardening Success with Difficult Soils.* Dallas, TX: Taylor Publishing. 1992.

Olkowski, Olkowski and Daar. *Common Sense Pest Control.* Newtown, CT: Taunton Press. 1991.

Osborne, Robert. *Hardy Roses.* Pownal, VT: Storey Communications. 1991.

Oster, Maggie. *The Rose Book.* Emmaus, PA: Rodale Press. 1994.

Parsons, Samuel B. *The Rose: Its History, Poetry, Culture, and Classification.* New York, NY: John Wiley. 1847.

Phillips, Roger and Rix, Martyn. *The Quest for the Rose.* New York, NY: Random House. 1993.

The River Oaks Garden Club. *A Garden Book for Houston and the Gulf Coast.* Houston, TX: Pacesetter Press. Revised edition 1979.

Rohde, Eleanour Sinclair. *Rose Recipes.* London: Chiswick Press. 1939.

Rodale, J. I., ed. *The Complete Book of Composting.* Emmaus, PA: Rodale Books. 1960.

Scanniello, Stephen and Bayard, Tania. *Climbing Roses.* New York, NY: Prentice Hall. 1994.

Scanniello, Stephen, ed. *Easy Care Roses.* Brooklyn, NY: Brooklyn Botanic Garden. 1995.

Sharpe, Margaret P. *Fun with Roses.* Houston, TX: self-published. 1986.

Smith, Leona Woodring. *The Forgotten Art of Flower Cookery.* Gretna, LA: Pelican. 1985.

Tompkins, Peter and Bird, Christopher. *Secrets of the Soil.* New York, NY: Harper & Row. 1989.

Verrier, Suzanne. *Rosa Rugosa.* Deer Park, WI: Capability's Books. 1991.

Walheim, Lance. *The Natural Rose Gardener.* Tucson, AZ: Ironwood Press. 1994.

Welch, William C. *Perennial Garden Color.* Dallas, TX: Taylor Publishing Company. 1989.

Welch, William C. *Antique Roses for the South.* Dallas, TX: Taylor Publishing Company. 1991.

Welch, William C., and Grant, Greg. *The Southern Heirloom Garden.* Dallas, TX: Taylor Publishing Company. 1995.

Westmacott, Richard. *African-American Garden and Yards in the Rural South.* Knoxville, TN: University of Tennessee Press. 1992.

INDEX

NOTE: Page numbers in *italics* refer to illustrations.

ABOUT THE AUTHOR

LIZ DRUITT is a garden writer, designer, consultant, and experienced Rose Rustler. She is the coauthor (with G. Michael Shoup) of the widely acclaimed *Landscaping with Antique Roses* and she worked with Elizabeth Winston to design and develop the ornamental organic gardens at the Organic Plant Institute (formerly the Peaceable Kingdom School). She's also a host on PBS's environmentally oriented gardening series *The New Garden.* Her gardening articles have appeared in *Fine Gardening, Flower and Garden,* and *Horticulture,* among other magazines. A board member of the Heritage Rose Foundation, Druitt lives in Pearland, Texas.